Title	Dewe©	Price

Publisher: Greenhaven Press
Library Binding
Reviews: ARBA

Gumdrop Price $1,826.70
Publisher's List Price $3,064.05

Explore current issues with expert opinions in a pro/con format and encourage critical thinking. Features a more user-friendly and visually appealing format than the original series.

Title	Dewey	©	Price
Labor Unions	331.8	12	$29.55
Marijuana	362.2	12	$29.55
Media Bias	302.2	11	$29.55
Middle East	956.0	07	$9.00
National Security	355	10	$29.45
Native Americans	305.8	08	$9.00
Nuclear Power	333.7	10	$29.45
Obesity	616.9	11	$29.45
Obesity	616.3	07	$9.00
Oceans	551.4	11	$29.55
Oil	553.2	08	$9.00
Organic Food and Farming	641.3	10	$29.55
Paranormal Phenomena	130	12	$29.55
Patriot Act	345.7	09	$9.00
Pollution	363.7	07	$9.00
Poverty	362.5	09	$9.00
Rap Music	306.4	08	$9.00
Religion in Schools	379.2	12	$29.55
School Policies	371.2	11	$29.55
Self Mutilation	616.8	09	$9.00
Sexually Transmitted Diseases	614.5	09	$9.00
Smoking	362.2	11	$29.55

Title	Dewey ©	Price
Standardized Testing	371.2	11	$29.55
Student Drug Testing	371.7	12	$29.55
Teen Sex	306.7	12	$29.55
Torture	364.6	11	$29.55
U.S. Economy	330.9	11	$29.55
UFOs	001.9	06	$9.00
Video Games	793.9	11	$29.55
Violence	303.6	10	$9.00
War	355.0	10	$29.45
Water Resource Management	333.9	08	$9.00
Welfare	362.5	09	$29.45
Women's Rights	305.4	10	$29.45

GD FIELD : 8/8/2012 (6x8.5)   **USD**

INTRODUCING
ISSUES WITH
OPPOSING
VIEWPOINTS®

Labor Unions

Noël Merino, *Book Editor*

GREENHAVEN PRESS
A part of Gale, Cengage Learning

GALE
CENGAGE Learning·

Detroit • New York • San Francisco • New Haven, Conn • Waterville, Maine • London

Elizabeth Des Chenes, *Director, Publishing Solutions*

For more information, contact:
Greenhaven Press
27500 Drake Rd.
Farmington Hills, MI 48331-3535
Or you can visit our Internet site at gale.cengage.com

For product information and technology assistance, contact us at

Gale Customer Support, 1-800-877-4253
For permission to use material from this text or product, submit all requests online at www.cengage.com/permissions

Further permissions questions can be e-mailed to permissionrequest@cengage.com

Articles in Greenhaven Press anthologies are often edited for length to meet page requirements. In addition, original titles of these works are changed to clearly present the main thesis and to explicitly indicate the author's opinion. Every effort is made to ensure that Greenhaven Press accurately reflects the original intent of the authors. Every effort has been made to trace the owners of copyrighted material.

Cover image © Kuzma/Shutterstock.com

LIBRARY OF CONGRESS CATALOGING-IN-PUBLICATION DATA

Labor unions / Noël Merino, book editor.
    p. cm. -- (Introducing issues with opposing viewpoints)
  Includes bibliographical references and index.
  ISBN 978-0-7377-6030-9 (hbk.)
  1. Labor unions--United States. I. Merino, Noël.
  HD6508.L235 2012
  331.880973--dc23

                                                                    2011047673

Printed in the United States of America
1 2 3 4 5 6 7 16 15 14 13 12

Contents

Foreword   5

Introduction   7

Chapter 1: What Is the Status of US Labor Unions?

1. Positive Attitudes Toward Labor Unions Have Fallen   11
   in Recent Years
   Akito Yoshikane

2. Americans Are Increasingly Recognizing   17
   the Benefits of Unions
   Dave Johnson

3. Labor Unions Harm the Overall Economy   23
   James Sherk

4. Labor Unions Do Not Harm State Economies   29
   Richard Florida

5. Labor Unions Have Tremendous Political Influence   36
   Peyton R. Miller

6. Labor Unions Have Become Progressively Less Influential   42
   Palash R. Ghosh

Chapter 2: Should Government Regulate Labor Unions?

1. States Should Repeal Collective Bargaining in the Public Sector   50
   Chris Edwards

2. Collective Bargaining Is a Right in Both the Private   56
   and Public Sectors
   Garrett Keizer

3. Right-to-Work Laws Protect Workers from Forced Unionization   61
   Bruce Walker

4. Right-to-Work Laws Aim to Reduce the Bargaining Power   66
   of Workers
   Dean Baker

5. The Employee Free Choice Act Should Be Passed   72
   AFL-CIO

6. The Employee Free Choice Act Should Not Be Passed   79
   Doug Bandow

Chapter 3: What Is the Future of Labor Unions?

1. A Political War Is Being Waged to Eliminate Labor Unions   86
   Jane McAlevey

2. Labor Unions' Decline Is Due to Their Anticompetitive Nature   93
   Daniel Griswold

3. America Needs Labor Unions to Counteract the Power   99
   of Big Business
   David Macaray

4. The US Economy Would Be Harmed by   105
   Increased Unionization
   Lee E. Ohanian

5. Attacks on Unions Have Drawn Public Sympathy   110
   Harold Meyerson

6. The Outlook for Private and Public Unions Is Bleak   115
   Michael Barone

Facts About Labor Unions   120
Organizations to Contact   122
For Further Reading   126
Index   131
Picture Credits   137

Foreword

Indulging in a wide spectrum of ideas, beliefs, and perspectives is a critical cornerstone of democracy. After all, it is often debates over differences of opinion, such as whether to legalize abortion, how to treat prisoners, or when to enact the death penalty, that shape our society and drive it forward. Such diversity of thought is frequently regarded as the hallmark of a healthy and civilized culture. As the Reverend Clifford Schutjer of the First Congregational Church in Mansfield, Ohio, declared in a 2001 sermon, "Surrounding oneself with only like-minded people, restricting what we listen to or read only to what we find agreeable is irresponsible. Refusing to entertain doubts once we make up our minds is a subtle but deadly form of arrogance." With this advice in mind, Introducing Issues with Opposing Viewpoints books aim to open readers' minds to the critically divergent views that comprise our world's most important debates.

Introducing Issues with Opposing Viewpoints simplifies for students the enormous and often overwhelming mass of material now available via print and electronic media. Collected in every volume is an array of opinions that captures the essence of a particular controversy or topic. Introducing Issues with Opposing Viewpoints books embody the spirit of nineteenth-century journalist Charles A. Dana's axiom: "Fight for your opinions, but do not believe that they contain the whole truth, or the only truth." Absorbing such contrasting opinions teaches students to analyze the strength of an argument and compare it to its opposition. From this process readers can inform and strengthen their own opinions, or be exposed to new information that will change their minds. Introducing Issues with Opposing Viewpoints is a mosaic of different voices. The authors are statesmen, pundits, academics, journalists, corporations, and ordinary people who have felt compelled to share their experiences and ideas in a public forum. Their words have been collected from newspapers, journals, books, speeches, interviews, and the Internet, the fastest growing body of opinionated material in the world.

Introducing Issues with Opposing Viewpoints shares many of the well-known features of its critically acclaimed parent series, Opposing Viewpoints. The articles are presented in a pro/con format, allowing readers to absorb divergent perspectives side by side. Active reading questions preface each viewpoint, requiring the student to approach the material thoughtfully and carefully. Useful charts, graphs, and cartoons supplement each article. A thorough introduction provides readers with crucial background on an issue. An annotated bibliography points the reader toward articles, books, and websites that contain additional information on the topic. An appendix of organizations to contact contains a wide variety of charities, nonprofit organizations, political groups, and private enterprises that each hold a position on the issue at hand. Finally, a comprehensive index allows readers to locate content quickly and efficiently.

Introducing Issues with Opposing Viewpoints is also significantly different from Opposing Viewpoints. As the series title implies, its presentation will help introduce students to the concept of opposing viewpoints, and learn to use this material to aid in critical writing and debate. The series' four-color, accessible format makes the books attractive and inviting to readers of all levels. In addition, each viewpoint has been carefully edited to maximize a reader's understanding of the content. Short but thorough viewpoints capture the essence of an argument. A substantial, thought-provoking essay question placed at the end of each viewpoint asks the student to further investigate the issues raised in the viewpoint, compare and contrast two authors' arguments, or consider how one might go about forming an opinion on the topic at hand. Each viewpoint contains sidebars that include at-a-glance information and handy statistics. A Facts About section located in the back of the book further supplies students with relevant facts and figures.

Following in the tradition of the Opposing Viewpoints series, Greenhaven Press continues to provide readers with invaluable exposure to the controversial issues that shape our world. As John Stuart Mill once wrote: "The only way in which a human being can make some approach to knowing the whole of a subject is by hearing what can be said about it by persons of every variety of opinion and studying all modes in which it can be looked at by every character of mind. No wise man ever acquired his wisdom in any mode but this." It is to this principle that Introducing Issues with Opposing Viewpoints books are dedicated.

Introduction

"Employees shall have the right to self-organization, to form, join, or assist labor organizations, to bargain collectively through representatives of their own choosing, and to engage in other concerted activities for the purpose of collective bargaining or other mutual aid or protection."

—National Labor Relations Act, 29 USC §157

Labor unions developed in the United States in the eighteenth and nineteenth centuries in response to low wages, long hours, and poor working conditions. A labor union is an organization of workers formed in order to protect their collective interests in the workplace. Labor unions exercise power by engaging in collective bargaining, strikes, and political activity. The primary activity of labor unions is bargaining with employers on behalf of their members. The union and the employer bargain about wages, hours, working conditions, hiring policies, and disciplinary policies. When agreement cannot be reached, unions may conduct a strike—stopping work in protest—in order to get the employer to meet their demands.

The right to form and join a union is protected by law in the United States. In 1935 Congress passed the National Labor Relations Act (NLRA), also called the Wagner Act, which recognized the right of workers to organize and bargain collectively with their employer. It also prevents employers from interfering with the efforts by employees to unionize or collectively bargain. The National Labor Relations Board (NLRB) was established to help guarantee the rights of employees to unionize, and it conducts elections for labor union representation and investigates complaints about unfair labor practices. An employer commits an unfair labor practice under the NLRA when it discriminates against, interferes with, or coerces its employees who are attempting to exercise their rights or when the employer refuses to bargain with a union that represents its employees.

The NLRA applies to employees of private businesses, but state law governs the union rights of public employees. States vary in their protection of the rights of public employees to unionize. The majority of states allow public employees to engage in collective bargaining, but some forbid it whereas others allow public employees to unionize but forbid striking.

Except where it is forbidden for public employees, workers can decide to form a labor union by getting a majority of employees to vote for representation by a union. Membership policies used in businesses where unions exist vary. With a union-shop policy, all workers must join the union when a majority of the workers choose a union to represent them. In contrast, an agency-shop policy allows union and nonunion workers to be employed, but nonunion employees must still pay union dues since the union represents all workers. This differs from an open-shop policy, which allows union and nonunion workers to be employed without requiring nonunion workers to pay dues, even though a union may sometimes represent all workers.

Different states have different laws regarding the ability of labor unions to operate. The 1947 Taft-Hartley Act allows states to pass laws that prohibit a union-shop policy and agency-shop policy for private and public workers alike. In fact, twenty-two states now have laws—known as right-to-work laws—that prohibit unions from forcing employees to join a union or to pay union dues, thus only allowing unions to operate with an open-shop policy. Right-to-work laws continue to be a source of controversy, with opponents such as the American Federation of Labor and Congress of Industrial Organizations (AFL-CIO) arguing against such laws: "To set the record (and the name) straight, right to work for less doesn't guarantee any rights. In fact, by weakening unions and collective bargaining, it destroys the best job security protection that exists: the union contract. Meanwhile, it allows workers to pay nothing and get all the benefits of union membership."

Proponents of such laws, such as the National Right to Work Committee, believe the laws protect the rights of workers: "State Right to Work laws (now 22 in number) greatly mitigate the harm caused by federally-sanctioned union monopoly. These laws protect private-sector employees from being fired under the forced-dues provisions in federal labor law. They also bar forced-union tribute in state and local government employment."

Unions are much less powerful and pervasive in right-to-work states, which some charge is resulting in companies choosing to move to right-to-work states in order to avoid dealing with unions.

In April 2011 the NLRB issued a complaint against the Boeing Company, alleging that Boeing's decision in 2009 to build a 787 Dreamliner assembly line in South Carolina rather than keep all 787 airplane assembly in Washington State constituted an illegal violation of the NLRA by retaliating against employees for exercising their legal collective bargaining rights. International Association of Machinist (IAM) union employees at Boeing in Washington complained to the NLRB that their past exercise of collective bargaining rights, including strikes, was the reason Boeing decided to relocate assembly to South Carolina, a state that—unlike Washington—has a right-to-work law. As of this writing, Republicans in the House of Representatives are advancing legislation (HR 2587) to attempt to "prohibit the National Labor Relations Board (NRLB) from ordering any employer to close, relocate, or transfer employment under any circumstance."

The ongoing issue with the Boeing Company is just one of the many battles being waged in today's society over the role of labor unions. Disagreement abounds about whether labor unions help or hurt the economy and whether government should make it easier or harder for labor unions to operate. The future of labor unions in the United States is unknown. A variety of viewpoints on the current status of labor unions, government regulation of unions, and the future of organized labor are included in *Introducing Issues with Opposing Viewpoints: Labor Unions.*

Chapter 1

What Is the Status of US Labor Unions?

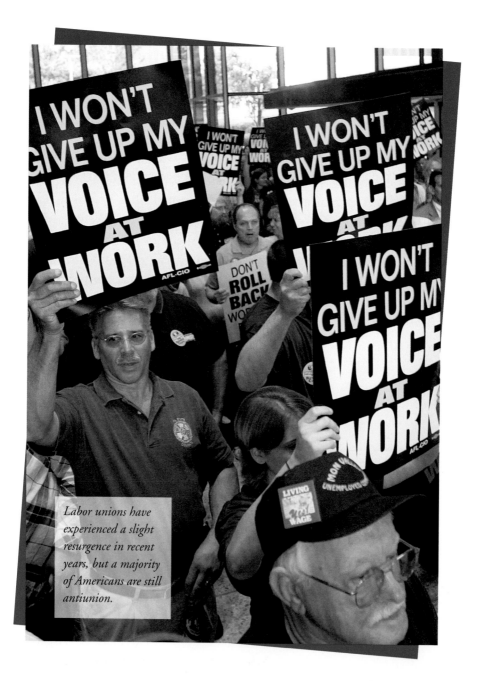

Labor unions have experienced a slight resurgence in recent years, but a majority of Americans are still antiunion.

Positive Attitudes Toward Labor Unions Have Fallen in Recent Years

"Positive attitudes toward unions have fallen in most demographic groups."

Akito Yoshikane

In the following viewpoint Akito Yoshikane argues that labor unions have lost public support among all segments of society, especially among senior citizens. Yoshikane contends that the reasons positive attitudes toward unions have declined are that union legislation has been stalled in Congress and unions have been subject to bad public relations. Yoshikane concludes that unions face unique challenges in a bad economy, and he claims unions need to do a better job of getting their message across if they are to improve their image. Yoshikane is a journalist based in New York City.

AS YOU READ, CONSIDER THE FOLLOWING QUESTIONS:
  1. According to Yoshikane, by how many percentage points did
     favorable attitudes toward unions drop from 2007 to 2010?
  2. What piece of labor legislation was put aside in order to pass the
     health care bill, according to the author?
  3. The author contends that the Pew Research Center survey on
     labor unions did not include what two groups?

U nions are losing the public-relations battle. A survey released
    [February 23, 2010,] by the Pew Research Center found that
    public approval of labor unions has declined significantly dur-
ing the last three years.

A Decline in Positive Attitudes

Positive attitudes toward unions have fallen in most demographic
groups. Forty-one percent of those surveyed say they have a favorable
view of labor unions, while nearly the same amount has an unfavorable view at 42 percent. The results are a *17-percent decline* from the
last poll taken in January 2007, when a majority of people (58 percent) had a good view of unions while 31 percent thought otherwise.
(The findings reinforce a 2009 Gallup poll that said only 48 percent
of Americans approve of labor unions—an all-time low since 1936.)

With private sector unionization rates continuing to decline in a
scarce job market and unemployment at record highs, unions are
somehow managing to lose mass appeal even as Americans face more
workplace challenges than ever.

The Pew survey, conducted from February 3 [to] 9, found that
regardless of race, gender, education level, income and political affiliation, each of these social groups saw a drop in union attitudes. The
largest change, 31 percent, came from those over the age of 65.

The new findings are a follow-up to another survey that suggested
people have grown skeptical about labor's purpose and rising influence.
A similar Pew survey from last April [2009] found that Americans were
less receptive to the idea that unions can protect working people. They
also expressed concern that unions "have too much power."

The results are bad news for a struggling labor movement, but what's the reason for the falling public support?

The Reason for Falling Support

Recently, unions have faced several legislative hurdles that have ostensibly stifled their capacity to improve American lives. In some cases, anti-union politicians have cast organized labor as a hindrance to economic growth.

Labor's achievements in Washington haven't measured up to expectations. Passing the Employee Free Choice Act was put on the shelf to make way for a sub-par healthcare bill. The confirmation of [union lawyer] Craig Becker to a seat on the National Labor Relations Board

In 2010 the Pew Research Center released a survey reporting that 59 percent of African Americans said they had a positive view of unions, down from 75 percent in 2007.

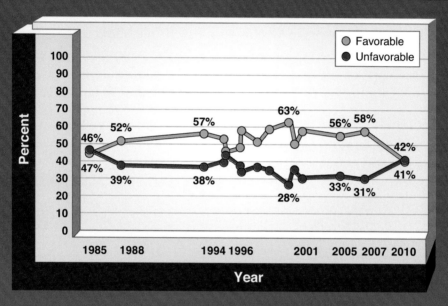

Labor Union Favorability Lowest Since 1985

Taken from: "Favorable Ratings of Labor Unions Fall Sharply." The Pew Research Center for the People and the Press, February 23, 2010.

was thwarted. Even with the president's ear [Democrat Barack Obama] and, until recently, a 60-vote Democratic majority in the Senate, unions have struggled to ease the burden for working people as key pieces of labor's legislative agendas remain stalled.

Similarly, unions have been subject to bad PR [public relations]. The perception exists that unions have become so powerful that high wages and benefits have stifled recovery. UAW's [United Auto Workers'] "jobs bank" was criticized for impeding carmakers' pleas for federal assistance; a strong teachers union makes it difficult to fire incompetent staff. As we've reported, the job losses in heavily unionized sectors in manufacturing and construction hurt membership.

Meanwhile, unions in the public sector have grown. But the increase in public union jobs could draw ire from taxpayers who could accuse state workers (and their pensions) for draining resources in the midst of budget shortfalls.

That may explain why nobody is as happy about unions as they were three years ago [in 2007]. Republicans, Independents and Democrats had similar patterns as favorable union opinions declined and unfavorable opinions rose. Democrats were still the most optimistic, though, with 56 percent still holding positive views, but it was a drop from 70 percent in 2007; unfavorable opinions rose from 19 to 26 percent.

A Delicate Balance

The findings might be grim, but one wonders if the statistics would have been better if the survey were more racially inclusive. Pew says both whites and African Americans saw declines in favorability to different degrees. White men in particular lost faith in unions. Meanwhile, a majority of African Americans still view unions in a positive light, just as they did three years ago but to a lesser extent.

Curiously though, the survey did not include Latinos and Asian Americans. It would have been interesting to see how their responses impacted the survey, considering that both groups are joining labor unions and enjoying greater benefits and wages than non-union members, according to reports by Center for Economic and Policy Research.

> **FAST FACT**
>
> A 2010 Pew Research Center survey reports that 59 percent of African Americans said they had a positive view of labor unions in 2010, down from 75 percent in 2007.

In this brutal economy, unions have the difficult task of orchestrating a delicate balance: By appearing intransigent in their demands, they risk coming off as too greedy with employers amid a recession. On the other hand, they also have to preserve the interests of their members by avoiding massive concessions.

Nevertheless, companies are using the recession to push unions and workers to make drastic concessions in wages and benefits. Labor has been fighting to improve working people's lives, but they clearly have a lot of work in getting their message across to the public.

EVALUATING THE AUTHOR'S ARGUMENTS:

In this viewpoint Akito Yoshikane contends that support for labor unions fell from 2007 to 2010. What new evidence from 2011 does Dave Johnson, author of the following viewpoint, give that may suggest that public opinion is becoming more favorable?

Viewpoint 2

Americans Are Increasingly Recognizing the Benefits of Unions

Dave Johnson

"America is waking up to the value of unions."

In the following viewpoint Dave Johnson argues that public opinion toward labor unions is improving. Johnson contends that the movement by the state of Wisconsin to restrict the collective bargaining rights of public-employee unions is opposed by most Americans. Furthermore, Johnson claims that the issue has brought the subject of labor unions to the forefront of the media, causing Americans to connect the dots and see how labor unions are good for wages, benefits, and working conditions. Johnson is a fellow at Campaign for America's Future, a progressive public policy research organization, in which capacity he writes about American manufacturing, trade, and economic/industrial policy. He is also a senior fellow with Renew California, a political action group.

A s Abraham Lincoln famously said, "You can fool some of the people all of the time, and all of the people some of the time, but you cannot fool all of the people all of the time." When you put enough dots in front of people sooner or later they will connect the dots. And Americans are connecting the dots.

The Value of Unions

Dots: Trade deals close factories, outsource jobs and pit workers against each other, then wages decline and unemployment is really high, while all the money goes to a few at the top. Then calls to cut the wages and benefits of the rest.

Dots: Unions squashed, then pensions disappear, then calls to get rid of public-employee unions *because they have pensions.*

Dots: Tax cuts for the rich, then panic over resulting deficits, then calls for cuts in the things government does for We, the People.

People are connecting the dots: *Unions mean better wages, benefits and working conditions.*

There is a joke circulating that goes like this:

A unionized public employee, a member of the Tea Party and a Big Corp [corporation] CEO are sitting at a table. In the middle of the table there is a plate with a dozen cookies on it. The CEO reaches across and takes 11 cookies, looks at the tea partier and says, "Look out for that union guy, he wants a piece of your cookie."

The situation in Wisconsin is waking America up to the value of unions. At a time when so many of us are hurting, seeing this naked attempt to strip from Wisconsin's public employees the ability to bargain for a better life is resonating. A CBS/*NY Times* poll finds that "a majority of Americans say they oppose efforts to weaken the collective bargaining rights of public employee unions and are also against cutting the pay or benefits of public workers to reduce state budget deficits."

Further down in the story, "Americans oppose weakening the bargaining rights of public employee unions by a margin of nearly two to one: 60 percent to 33 percent."

On how to fix budget deficits, "those polled preferred tax increases over benefit cuts for state workers by nearly two to one."

Thousands of Wisconsinites demonstrate at the state capitol in Madison on February 26, 2011. Governor Scott Walker's attempt to strip public employees of their collective bargaining rights has galvanized the US labor movement.

Americans Weigh in on Labor Unions and Public Employees

Collective bargaining refers to negotiations between an employer and a labor union's members to determine the conditions of employment. Some states are trying to take away some of the collective bargaining rights of public-employee unions. Do you favor or oppose taking away some of the collective bargaining rights of these unions?

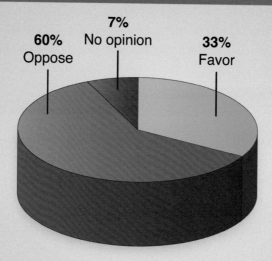

60% Oppose   **7%** No opinion   **33%** Favor

Taken from: *New York Times*/CBS News Poll, February 24–27, 2011.

Labor Unions in the Media

Interestingly, though, from the polling story, "Labor unions are not exactly popular, though: A third of those surveyed viewed them favorably, a quarter viewed them unfavorably, and the rest said they were either undecided or had not heard enough about them."

Wow! More than 1/3 of the public hasn't heard enough about unions to know if they like them or not! *This is not surprising: When was the last time you read, saw or heard from a union in the major media, explaining the benefits of joining a union?* There has been a virtual blackout of information about unions in the corporate media.

So this Wisconsin story is bringing home to people that there is this thing called "collective bargaining" that can help them in their own jobs!

The plan was to spend a year claiming that public employees and their pensions were responsible for state budget deficits, then go after the unions. The strategy also threw in a dose of resentment: People were reminded that their pensions were stolen in the 80's, but these uppity gubment workers still had pensions, so their pensions should be stolen too! But people are smarter than the plutocrats think, and they connected some more dots:

Dot: People in unions have good wages and benefits including pensions.

Well, that's only one dot, but it doesn't take a lot of neuron connections to realize this means that you should join a union, not be against unions! The resentment argument backfired, and people are waking up to the value of unions.

The Reagan Revolution

Since the [former president Ronald] Reagan Revolution crushed unions, wages for everyone except a few at the top have been flat. In the [George] 'W' Bush decade even before the financial crash, wages were declining and job growth was anemic. And wages have been stagnant since this "recovery" began.

This wage stagnation is the result of of the loss of the bargaining power of working people.

Working people's share of the benefits from increased productivity took a sudden [downturn] when the Reagan Revolution crushed unions: Wage stagnation resulted.

Unions are vital to a middle-class society. Corporations and the wealthy behind the corporate mask have so much power. The only forces that can counter that

FAST FACT

In March 2011 the Wisconsin legislature passed a bill limiting the collective bargaining rights of public employees and ending the state's collection of union dues.

power and fight for the rest of us are the unions and democratic government. The Reagan Revolution began the elimination of both, bringing instead plutocracy—government of, by and for the wealthy. The resulting weakness in the power of working people to bargain for a fair share has left us with an economy that didn't work when it was "recovering" under Bush, and now can't get out of the recession. To lift the economy we have to lift wages.

Families are not sharing in the rewards, but they are waking up and connecting the dots. America is waking up to the value of unions.

EVALUATING THE AUTHOR'S ARGUMENTS:

In this viewpoint Dave Johnson contends that although almost two-thirds of Americans largely oppose the weakening of the collective bargaining rights of public-employee unions, only a third view labor unions favorably. How does Johnson explain this apparent contradiction? Suggest an alternate explanation for the two contrasting poll results.

Labor Unions Harm the Overall Economy

"While unions can sometimes achieve benefits for their members, they harm the overall economy."

James Sherk

In the following viewpoint James Sherk argues that empirical research confirms economic theory showing that labor unions raise wages at the cost of profits and jobs, harming the economy. Sherk contends that labor unions artificially restrict the number of workers in order to drive up wages, at the expense of future business investment. Sherk claims that higher wages secured by union members are the result of lower profits for the business or higher prices for consumers, both of which he claims harm the economy. Sherk is senior policy analyst in labor economics at the Heritage Foundation's Center for Data Analysis.

AS YOU READ, CONSIDER THE FOLLOWING QUESTIONS:
1. Sherk argues that economic research shows unions benefit their members but hurt whom?
2. According to the author, how do cartels work?
3. What effect does competition have on the union cartel, according to Sherk?

What do unions do? The AFL-CIO [American Federation of Labor and Congress of Industrial Organizations] argues that unions offer a pathway to higher wages and prosperity for the middle class. Critics point to the collapse of many highly unionized domestic industries and argue that unions harm the economy. To whom should policymakers listen? What unions do has been studied extensively by economists, and a broad survey of academic studies shows that while unions can sometimes achieve benefits for their members, they harm the overall economy.

The Effect of Unions on Jobs

Unions function as labor cartels [a group formed to regulate pricing, production, or other economic factors]. A labor cartel restricts the number of workers in a company or industry to drive up the remaining workers' wages, just as the Organization of Petroleum Exporting Countries (OPEC) attempts to cut the supply of oil to raise its price.

FAST FACT

Studies by economists have found that unionized companies earn profits between 10 and 15 percent lower than comparable nonunion companies.

Companies pass on those higher wages to consumers through higher prices, and often they also earn lower profits. Economic research finds that unions benefit their members but hurt consumers generally, and especially workers who are denied job opportunities.

The average union member earns more than the average nonunion worker. However, that does not mean that expanding union membership will raise wages: Few workers who join a union today get a pay raise. What explains these apparently contradictory findings? The economy has become more competitive over the past generation. Companies have less power to pass price increases on to consumers without going out of business. Consequently, unions do not negotiate higher wages for many newly organized workers. These days, unions win higher wages for employees only at companies with competitive advantages that allow them to pay higher wages, such as

Total manufacturing employment has declined steadily over the past generation because of the loss of union jobs. Three-fourths of union manufacturing jobs have disappeared over the past thirty years. Total nonunion manufacturing jobs increased slightly over that time.

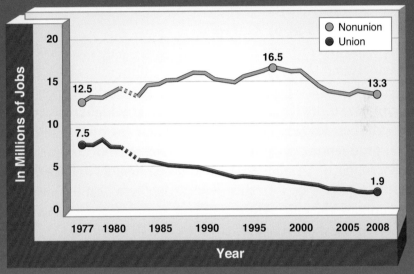

Note: Data for 1982 not available from Bureau of Labor Statistics.

Taken from: James Sherk. "What Unions Do: How Labor Unions Affect Jobs and the Economy." *Backgrounder*, no. 2275, May 21, 2009.

successful research and development (R&D) projects or capital investments.

Unions effectively tax these investments by negotiating higher wages for their members, thus lowering profits. Unionized companies respond to this union tax by reducing investment. Less investment makes unionized companies less competitive.

This, along with the fact that unions function as labor cartels that seek to reduce job opportunities, causes unionized companies to lose jobs. Economists consistently find that unions decrease the number of jobs available in the economy. The vast majority of manufacturing jobs lost over the past three decades have been among union members —non-union manufacturing employment has risen. Research also shows that widespread unionization delays recovery from economic downturns.

Some unions win higher wages for their members, though many do not. But with these higher wages, unions bring less investment, fewer jobs, higher prices, and smaller 401(k) plans for everyone else. On balance, labor cartels harm the economy, and enacting policies designed to force workers into unions will only prolong the recession. . . .

The Impact of Labor Cartels

Unions argue that they can raise their members' wages, but few Americans understand the economic theory explaining how they do this. Unions are labor cartels. Cartels work by restricting the supply of what they produce so that consumers will have to pay higher prices for it. OPEC, the best-known cartel, attempts to raise the price of oil by cutting oil production. As labor cartels, unions attempt to monopolize the labor supplied to a company or an industry in order to force employers to pay higher wages. In this respect, they function like any other cartel and have the same effects on the economy. Cartels benefit their members in the short run and harm the overall economy.

Imagine that General Motors [GM], Ford, and Chrysler jointly agreed to raise the price of the cars they sold by $2,000: Their profits would rise as every American who bought a car paid more. Some Americans would no longer be able to afford a car at the higher price, so the automakers would manufacture and sell fewer vehicles. Then they would need—and hire—fewer workers. The Detroit automakers' stock prices would rise, but the overall economy would suffer. That is why federal anti-trust laws prohibit cartels and the automakers cannot collude to raise prices.

Now consider how the United Auto Workers (UAW)—the union representing the autoworkers in Detroit—functions. Before the current downturn, the UAW routinely went on strike unless the Detroit automakers paid what they demanded—until recently, $70 an hour in wages and benefits. Gold-plated UAW health benefits for retirees and active workers added $1,200 to the cost of each vehicle that GM produced in 2007. Other benefits, such as full retirement after 30 years of employment and the recently eliminated JOBS bank (which paid workers for not working), added more.

Some of these costs come out of profits, and some get passed to consumers through higher prices. UAW members earn higher wages, but every American who buys a car pays more, stock owners' wealth falls, and some Americans can no longer afford to buy a new car. The automakers also hire fewer workers because they now make and sell fewer cars.

An autoworker works on a car at the General Motors assembly plant in Hamtramck, Michigan. According to union opponents, the United Auto Workers union has hurt the auto industry financially due to the high wages and strong benefits provided to union workers.

The Unions as Monopolies

Unions raise the wages of their members both by forcing consumers to pay more for what they buy or do without and by costing some workers their jobs. They have the same harmful effect on the economy as other cartels, despite benefiting some workers instead of stock owners. That is why the federal anti-trust laws exempt labor unions; otherwise, anti-monopoly statutes would also prohibit union activity.

Unions' role as monopoly cartels explains their opposition to trade and competition. A cartel can charge higher prices only as long as it remains a monopoly. If consumers can buy elsewhere, a company must cut its prices or go out of business.

This has happened to the UAW. Non-union workers at Honda and Toyota plants [outside the United States] now produce high-quality cars at lower prices than are possible in Detroit [Michigan]. As consumers have voted with their feet, the Detroit automakers have been brought to the brink of bankruptcy. The UAW has now agreed to significant concessions that will eliminate a sizeable portion of the gap between UAW and non-union wages. With competition, the union cartel breaks down, and unions cannot force consumers to pay higher prices or capture higher wages for their members.

Economic theory consequently suggests that unions raise the wages of their members at the cost of lower profits and fewer jobs, that lower profits cause businesses to invest less, and that unions have a smaller effect in competitive markets (where a union cannot obtain a monopoly). Dozens of economic studies have examined how unions affect the economy, and empirical research largely confirms the results of economic theory.

EVALUATING THE AUTHOR'S ARGUMENTS:

In this viewpoint James Sherk argues that labor unions harm the economy. What piece of economic evidence does Richard Florida, author of the following viewpoint, present that appears to undermine Sherk's thesis?

Viewpoint

4

Labor Unions Do Not Harm State Economies

Richard Florida

"Unions are not the cause of the serious economic and fiscal problems that are challenging so many American states."

In the following viewpoint Richard Florida argues that the existence of unions does not appear to affect state economies negatively. Florida considers the rates of union membership in the fifty states, noting that the union membership levels vary widely among states. Assessing the economies of states with high union membership against those with low union membership, Florida claims that union membership is moderately correlated with higher wages, lower hours worked, fewer working-class jobs, and more creative jobs. He concludes that the existence of labor unions has little to do with state budget problems. Florida is senior editor at the *Atlantic* and director of the Martin Prosperity Institute at the University of Toronto.

AS YOU READ, CONSIDER THE FOLLOWING QUESTIONS:
1 According to Florida, what percentage of workers nationally are union members?
2. Florida claims that unionization is correlated with which of the following: higher incomes across the board or lower incomes across the board?
3. What fraction of workers in the Rustbelt states—Michigan, Illinois, Pennsylvania, and Ohio—belong to a union, according to the author?

"The bitter political standoff in Wisconsin over Governor Scott Walker's bid to sharply curtail collective bargaining for public-sector workers ended abruptly [on March 9, 2011,] as Republican colleagues in the State Senate successfully maneuvered to adopt a bill doing just that," *The New York Times* report[ed the next morning]. "Democrats . . . condemned the move as an attack on working families, a violation of open meetings requirements . . . and a virtual firebomb in a state that already found itself politically polarized and consumed with recall efforts, large scale protests and fury from public workers." Rallies and demonstrations continue in the state.

The Rhetoric About Unions

As heated as it's been, the rhetoric over unions is fast-approaching the boiling point; Wisconsin is just the beginning. The right accuses unions, especially public sector unions, of stifling economic competitiveness and putting state economies in the red. "The bottom line is we are trying to balance our budget and there really is no room to negotiate on that because we're broke," Scott Walker told George Stephanopoulos on *Good Morning America*. Or as Harvard economist Robert Barro wrote in the *The Wall Street Journal*: "Labor unions like to portray collective bargaining as a basic civil liberty, akin to the freedoms of speech, press, assembly and religion . . . [but] collective bargaining on a broad scale is more similar to an antitrust violation than to a civil liberty."

On the left, unions are seen as a bulwark against falling wages and the decline of the middle class. "Collective bargaining didn't cause the economic meltdown, and crushing unions won't solve it," Paul Toner, the president of the Massachusetts Teachers Association, protested in *The Boston Globe.* In a passionate defense of unions on the op ed page of *The Washington Post,* Yale's Jacob S. Hacker and [University of California at] Berkeley's Paul Pierson pointed out that unions "have resisted the rampant deregulation of financial markets and the soaring growth of executive pay. They have been one of the few organized voices that has consistently pressed back against the string of tax-cut bills for the rich that began in the late 1970s."

For all the sound and fury, neither side has adduced much hard data to support their positions. While there have been many studies of the effects of unions on corporate profits and productivity, surprisingly few assess their effects on state economies. (One exception is a careful 1988 study by Harvard labor economist Richard Freeman, "Union Density and Economic Performance," which finds that union density improves earnings and income, but exacerbates unemployment and hurts growth.) But that was over twenty years ago. And so, with my colleagues at the Martin Prosperity Institute, I decided to take a close look at current data and trends for unions across the 50 states.

> ## FAST FACT
>
> The US Bureau of Labor Statistics reports that in 2010 full-time wage-earning and salaried union members had median weekly earnings of $917, whereas those workers not represented by unions had median weekly earnings of $717.

Union Membership Across the States

For starters, there's huge variation in unionization levels across the U.S. states. Nationally, nearly 12 percent (11.9%) of workers are union members. New York touts the highest level of unionization in the nation, more than double the national rate at 24.2% percent. More than one in five workers are union members in Alaska (22.9%) and Hawaii (21.8%). Unionization tops 15 percent in an additional ten states, and it's above 10 percent in 14 more. Wisconsin ranks 17th in union membership, less than 15 percent (14.2%) of its workforce are union members.

On the other side of the ledger, just 3.2 percent of North Carolina's workforce is unionized. Union members make up less than one in 20 workers in Georgia (4%), Arkansas (4%), Louisiana (4.3%), Mississippi (4.5%), Virginia and South Carolina (4.6%) and Tennessee (4.7%). While the conventional wisdom is that large numbers of workers are unionized in the Rustbelt states, that's more of a myth than reality. Less than one in five workers in Michigan (16.75%) belong to unions. The rate is 15.5% in Illinois, 14.7% in Pennsylvania, and 13.7% in Ohio.

Unionization has fallen off massively in the past fifty years or so. Part of this is doubtless due to the transformation of the American economy from one that was primarily industrial to one that is more knowledge and service based. Still the numbers are staggering.

Nationally, the percentage of union members declined by almost 20 percentage points (17.4) from 1964 to 2010. This drop has been much more pronounced in certain states, especially the older industrial states. Union membership fell by more than 30 percentage points in Indiana, from 40.8% to 10.9%; from 39.9% to 7.3% in New Jersey and from 36.5% to 4.6% in West Virginia. Ten additional states

Members of the Ohio Federation of Teachers union demonstrate at the state capitol in Columbus in March 2011. Nationally only 11.9 percent of teachers are unionized.

posted declines of 20 percent or more. Wisconsin saw its rate of union membership fall from 34 to 14 percent. And 25 others saw declines of more than ten percentage points.

Unions and State Economic Health

All the posturing and sound byte–ready rhetoric aside, how *do* unions line up against key measures of state economic health? Are more unionized states less competitive, as right wing critics would have us believe? Conversely, do unions provide a bulwark against unemployment and other adverse economic outcomes?

Relying on the steady statistical hand of my collaborator Charlotta Mellander, we examined the relationships between state unionization levels and key measures of state economies. As always, we remind our readers that correlation [where 0 shows no correlation, 1 shows a complete positive correlation, and -1 shows a complete negative correlation] is not causation—we are simply looking at associations. Nonetheless, they tell a very different story than the ones you're most likely to hear.

Unionized states are better-off economically than non-unionized states. While it's probably not surprising that unionization levels are correlated with higher hourly wages (.48), they are also correlated with higher incomes across the board—and the correlation between union membership and median income is substantial (.45). To put it baldly, unions are associated with the country's economic winners, not its losers. And it's not that unionized states work more—unionization is negatively correlated with hours worked (-.36). States with higher levels of union membership work less hours per week but make more money—higher levels of union memberships are positively correlated with wage per hour (.48).

That said, unionization does not appear to mitigate the effects of inequality or to protect against unemployment, according to our analysis. There is no correlation whatsoever between union membership and income inequality. Union membership is not correlated with unemployment, either.

Unions are usually thought to go along with blue-collar working class jobs. But that's not the case either, at least for state economies. Union membership is negatively correlated with the proportion of blue-collar, working class jobs in a state (-.48). This too is a likely consequence of

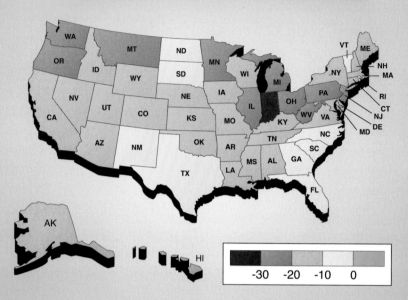

Change in Unionization, 1964–2010

-30   -20   -10   0

Taken from: Richard Florida. "Unions and State Economies: Don't Believe the Hype." *Atlantic*, March 10, 2011.

the ongoing transformation of the U.S. economy. As manufacturing unions have declined, service and public workers unions have grown.

To that point, unionization levels are higher in states with more highly educated workforces and knowledge based economies. Union membership is moderately correlated (.3) with both human capital levels (the percent of adults with a college degree) and the share of the workforce in knowledge, professional, and creative jobs (.35). More surprising, unionization is even more highly correlated with the percentage of the workforce in artistic and culturally creative jobs (.53). This is not to say that artistic and culturally creative workers are more likely to belong to unions (though some, like actors and musicians, do) but rather that states with more dynamic creative economies are also more likely to be highly unionized. It's also worth pointing out that unionization is more likely in states with higher levels of immigrants. Union membership is closely correlated with the share of adults that are foreign born (.42).

The Economic Influence of Unions

Unions continue to be a hot-button issue in American politics despite the fact that the level of unionization has fallen precipitously over the past half century. While many continue to think of unions as the province of blue-collar working class economies, less than one in five workers in Rustbelt states—Michigan, Illinois, Pennsylvania, Ohio—belongs to a union. Union states have more knowledge-intensive economies, boast more highly educated workforces, and have higher incomes as well.

The basic fact that unions are positively associated with so many key measures of prosperity suggests that their existence has little to do with state budget problems. Unions are not the cause of the serious economic and fiscal problems that are challenging so many American states, which are a result of the economic crisis, collapsed housing market and massively reduced revenues. In fact, the economic influence of unions has been dramatically curtailed as a result of the ongoing transformation of the U.S. economy. At the same time, the existence of unions does not appear to be enough to forestall growing income inequality within the U.S. states.

It's time to get beyond the angry, ideologically motivated rhetoric about unions. We need to put our fiscal house in order and buckle down to the serious business of generating good jobs; more than that, we need to reinvent the U.S. economy for this new age.

EVALUATING THE AUTHOR'S ARGUMENTS:

In this viewpoint Richard Florida argues that labor unions are not the reason for the economic struggles of states. Does Florida's argument refute James Sherk's claim in the previous viewpoint that labor unions harm the overall economy? Why or why not?

Labor Unions Have Tremendous Political Influence

Peyton R. Miller

"Organized labor contin- ues to wield tremendous political influence."

In the following viewpoint Peyton R. Miller argues that organized labor contributes millions in political donations to Democrats and has received pro-labor government appointments and legislation under the Barack Obama administration. Miller claims that even though the pro-union Employee Free Choice Act has not passed, pro-union regulations and legislation may end up effectively enacting its provisions. Miller concludes that unions are effective at lobbying for legislation that is not good for the rest of the country. Miller is the editor of the *Harvard Salient* and a Student Free Press Association intern at the *Weekly Standard.*

AS YOU READ, CONSIDER THE FOLLOWING QUESTIONS:
1. The author claims that President Obama appointed two pro-union members to what government agency?
2. Miller charges that the bailouts of General Motors and Chrysler gave preferential treatment to the United Auto Workers union over whom?
3. The author contends that the Democratic health care bill contained what pro-union component?

L abor union membership has declined dramatically in the past six decades, from over a third of the workforce in 1945 to just 7.2 percent of private sector employees in 2009; unions are now overwhelmingly concentrated in the public sector. But organized labor continues to wield tremendous political influence. Unions spent $400 million during the 2008 elections in support of Democratic candidates, and Barack Obama has been grateful.

An Increase in Pro-Union Government Leadership

While the president has failed to enact the Employee Free Choice Act (EFCA)—the mother of all pro-union legislation, which includes the infamous "card check" proposal [wherein employees sign forms, or cards, indicating their desire to be represented by a union] to effectively eliminate the secret ballot from union elections—he has made it possible for labor leaders to implement EFCA provisions by other means. Through the National Labor Relations Board (NLRB), for instance. The NLRB conducts union elections and remedies unfair labor practices in most industries; Obama has named two pro-union members to this body—both were radical enough to require recess appointments. Stewart Acuff of the Utility Workers Union of America vowed to the *Huffington Post* that even if EFCA does not pass, labor leaders will work with the president's NLRB appointees "to change the rules governing forming a union through administrative action." The board is now considering use of remote online voting rather than in-person ballots in representation elections, which like card check could expose workers to undue influence from organizers.

An Obama appointee to the National Mediation Board, which coordinates railroad and airline labor-management relations, precipitated a rule change in May [2010] to allow approval of union representation by a majority of those voting, rather than a majority of a company's entire workforce, as in the past. The U.S. Chamber of Commerce notes that the new rule violates the Railway Labor Act, which was designed to prevent a few disgruntled employees from triggering a strike that could cripple commerce throughout the country.

The Passage of Pro-Union Legislation

President Obama has unilaterally aided unions through regulatory initiatives, which, according to Randel Johnson of the U.S. Chamber of Commerce, have mirrored the "wish list" presented to the Obama transition team by the AFL-CIO [American Federation of Labor and Congress of Industrial Organizations]. Obama signed an executive order requiring federal contractors to inform employees of their right to organize under federal labor laws, and revoked an order that they be informed of their right to forgo joining a union or paying certain union dues. Another executive order reflected unions' preference for seniority-based hiring by requiring contractors to offer existing service employees first refusal of positions for which they are qualified under a new contract.

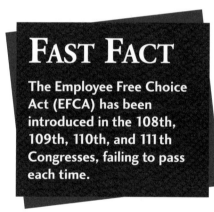

FAST FACT

The Employee Free Choice Act (EFCA) has been introduced in the 108th, 109th, 110th, and 111th Congresses, failing to pass each time.

Obama has precluded reimbursement of expenses contractors incur to influence employees' decision to form a union, and relaxed union financial disclosure requirements. He strongly encouraged federal agencies to award construction contracts of more than $25 million to companies that either employ unionized workers or offer union wages and benefits, which is bound to increase the cost of government construction.

The president's bailouts of General Motors and Chrysler subverted bankruptcy law by giving preferential treatment to the United Auto

The author asserts that President Barack Obama's executive orders concerning union-organizing rights of federal workers is proof that unions have too much political influence.

Workers [UAW] over the automakers' secured creditors. Bondholders ended up with a smaller stake than the UAW members of both companies, even though they had lent money under the contractual understanding that they would be compensated first in the event of bankruptcy.

Big Labor has also benefited from Obama's legislative agenda. He enacted a 35 percent tariff on Chinese tires at the behest of the United Steelworkers, fulfilled a Teamsters Union priority by canceling a program allowing Mexican trucks to carry cargo on American roads, and required that projects funded by the 2009 stimulus use U.S.-manufactured supplies.

The stimulus bill operates under the Davis-Bacon Act, which requires that employees of public works projects receive the prevailing wage in the area as determined by the Department of Labor. The regulation raises costs by putting a floor under wages for the more than 678,000 public construction jobs to be created by the end of 2010—many of which are in areas where Davis-Bacon has not previously applied. The bill also included a $53.6 billion "State Fiscal Stabilization Fund" to prevent layoffs of heavily unionized public employees.

The Impact of Union Advocacy

And labor unions have not been docile since 2008. They funded a multi-million-dollar "grassroots" effort to counteract opposition to Obamacare, whose mandates and subsidies will generate new demand for health services, and thus more dues-paying union members in the health sector. As J. Justin Wilson of the Center for Union Facts points out, the activism was also part of a broader advocacy of a federal beachhead in certain industries, which allows unions to lobby the government for favorable regulations. More directly, the Democratic health care bill included a $10 billion bailout of mismanaged retiree health plans that will benefit numerous former union workers.

"Placating the Unions . . . Chinese Tire Tariff," Nick Anderson's Editorial Cartoon used with the permission of Nick Anderson, the Washington Post Writers Group and the Cartoonist Group. All rights reserved.

Just last month [June 2010], Obama asked Congress for another $50 billion, on top of what the stimulus already provided, to prevent states from firing employees. While he's stopped campaigning for EFCA, the president may yet have an opportunity to sign it in some form. AFL-CIO president Richard Trumka is determined to see card check attached to an urgent bill while Democrats still have decisive congressional majorities. Democratic leaders have indicated that the lame duck session following the November [2010] elections may be the best opportunity.

Even if no other pro-union legislation comes to pass, President Obama has more than paid off big labor's $400 million investment, albeit at the expense of the rest of the country.

EVALUATING THE AUTHOR'S ARGUMENTS:

In this viewpoint Peyton R. Miller argues that unions have huge political influence. Based on the following viewpoint of Palash R. Ghosh, is this political influence likely to increase or decrease in coming years. Do you think Miller would agree with him? Why or why not?

Labor Unions Have Become Progressively Less Influential

Palash R. Ghosh

"Perhaps another ironic reason for the decline in U.S. unions has to do with the dynamic, fluid nature of the American labor and economy."

In the following viewpoint Palash R. Ghosh argues that labor unions are declining in popularity and influence for a number of reasons. Ghosh claims that one explanation for the decline of unions is the poor economy from the recession. Union membership has been falling because jobs with the highest unionization rates, such as manufacturing, are themselves in decline. Changes in industry, such as increased mechanization and laborsaving equipment, have also played a role in reducing union membership. However, while unions have lost much of their previous political clout, in regions of high membership unions may still be able to influence particular political races. Ghosh is a staff writer for the *International Business Times*, one of the world's leading business news organizations.

AS YOU READ, CONSIDER THE FOLLOWING QUESTIONS:
1. What percent of US workers did unions represent in the mid-1950s, as cited in the viewpoint?
2. What was the total union membership rate in the United States in 2009, according to Ghosh?
3. In the author's opinion, how has manufacturing played a role in reducing labor union membership?

A usterity measures by some European governments have elicited a wave of opposition, in some cases violence, from labor unions all over the continent. Demonstrations in Paris, Madrid and Athens have brought out millions of people enraged by their governments' draconian fiscal proposals. In some cases, public transport was completely shut down.

How successfully these protests can block their government programs and spending cuts will be interesting to see, but the ferocity of the unions' campaign in Europe presents a stark contrast to their counterparts on this side of the Atlantic, where the union movement seems to be gradually fading away.

U.S. Labor Unions Are in Decline

The unions in the U.S., which has provided American workers with the 40-hour work-week, minimum wage, paid vacations, health insurance, pensions, among other things, have been in steep decline for many decades due to a number of factors.

In their glory days, in the mid-1950s, unions represented about 35 percent of all U.S. workers—that figure has now been cut by two-thirds.

However, it is important to note that unions among public sector employees remains fairly strong. According to the Bureau of Labor Statistics (BLS), in 2009 the union membership rate for public sector workers came in at 37.4 percent, versus a figure of only 7.2 percent for private industry workers.

Interestingly, more public sector employees (7.9 million) belong to a union than did private sector employees (7.4 million), despite there being five times more workers in the private sector.

Americans' Approval of Labor Unions

Do you approve or disapprove of labor unions?

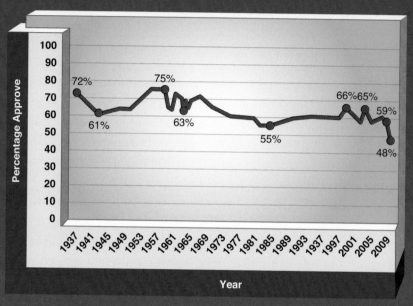

Taken from: Gallup Poll, August 6–9, 2009.

Also, the BLS said that the total union membership rate in the U.S. in 2009 amounted to 12.3 percent.

Workers in education, training, and library occupations had the highest unionization rate at 38.1 percent.

The Impact of the Recession

However, the absolute number of workers belonging to unions declined by 771,000 to 15.3 million, largely reflecting the overall drop in employment due to the recession.

"Union membership in the private sector has been steadily falling because the types of jobs that tended to have highest unionization rates, for example, durable goods manufacturing, are themselves in decline and now account for a smaller share of the overall economy," said Stephen Bronars, senior economist with Welch Consulting, a labor & employment consultancy in Washington D.C.

In addition, areas that have seen a large increase in population and job-growth over the past few decades—that is, the South, Southwest and West—have tended to discourage unionization (i.e., the "Right-to-Work" states).

"It's hard to establish unions in some of these places," Bronars said.

Indeed, the only thing keeping the American union movement alive, Bronars states, is the public sector unions.

"Groups like AFSCME, [American Federation of State, County, and Municipal Employees]which represents government employees of all levels, as well as many other service-oriented professions, remain pretty vibrant," he said.

The Impact of Manufacturing and Globalization

Indeed, the very nature of manufacturing has played a role in reducing union membership in the private sector.

"Unions have suffered losses in industries where there is more mechanization and labor-saving equipment," Bronars said.

"That is, a substitution of capital for labor occurred as labor costs got higher. The classic example of this is the auto industry, in which the numbers of jobs have fallen much more than production has. Auto plants now have fewer workers, but they are more productive than before. This concept really hasn't had as much of an impact on the public sector sphere, which tends to be more service-oriented."

But perhaps the biggest blow to the US union movement has been globalization.

"American workers are now in competition with literally billions of foreign workers, in places like China, India and Latin America, who work for a fraction of what Americans do," Bronars noted. "American unions just can't compete with low-cost foreign-made goods."

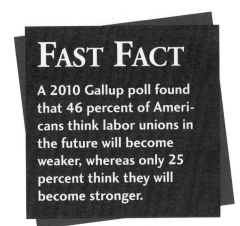

FAST FACT

A 2010 Gallup poll found that 46 percent of Americans think labor unions in the future will become weaker, whereas only 25 percent think they will become stronger.

Perhaps another ironic reason for the decline in U.S. unions has to do with the dynamic, fluid nature of the American labor and economy.

"Salaries within particular industries in the U.S. are not standardized, like they usually are in Europe," Bronars said.

"If a worker is unhappy with his rate of pay, he may choose to move to another area and find work in his field that offers higher wages."

This freedom of movement tends to deflate union power; whereas in Europe, the pay rate is standardized across the same industry and it's a little harder to pull up stakes and move.

American Unions Are Losing Political Influence

American unions also have appeared to have lost much of their once-vaunted political influence.

For example, unions strongly opposed the candidacy of Blanche Lincoln in Arkansas earlier this summer as she ran in a senate run-off contest. She won.

The Wagner Act was passed to make collective bargaining easier. The first test of the act came in 1937, when Pennsylvania steelworkers voted for a union to represent them in collective bargaining.

"That may not necessarily indicate a lessening of unions' political clouts because Arkansas is not at all a heavily-unionized state," Bronars noted. "I think that in regions of high union membership, unions may still be able to influence certain political races."

But it's clear that the days when national political candidates desperately sought the endorsement of the UAW [United Auto Workers] or AFL-CIO [American Federation of Labor and Congress of Industrial Organizations] are probably long gone.

But what about Europe? Are their unions stronger than their American peers?

Bronars explains that unions in France and Spain (two countries with a passionate opposition to government-enforced budget cuts) are organized and operated very differently from American unions.

"In some of the European countries the way the laws are set up, a union can negotiate the pay rates, working conditions, etc., for a whole industry or, in some cases, an entire region," he said. "This gives them much more power and influence than U.S. unions, where typically a union represents workers of just one company, not an entire industry."

Thus, even if a particular industry in France has only 15 percent union membership, more than 90 percent of the workers in that industry might be subject to the labor/collective bargaining agreements negotiated by that union.

Hence, the huge crowds of angry protesters carrying placards and bullhorns.

Of course, a qualitative judgment must also be made—the political activism among U.S. unions appears to be eroding, while unions in the United Kingdom [UK] and Europe remain forceful.

The Outlook for U.S. Unions

Bronars believes the outlook for the U.S. union movement is pretty bleak, at least for the private sector, given the huge shadows cast by globalization.

"The U.S. consumer looks at the bottom line, cheap prices, and that places the U.S. manufacturer at a great disadvantage," he said. "Manufacturing as a percentage of the overall economy and workforce continues to shrink, and this is the one industry which has traditionally had high union membership. I don't see a catalyst that will reinvigorate the union movement in the U.S."

However, Bronars adds that European unions also face many challenges, given the fragile, even dire, states of their national economies and high unemployment.

"Unions in Europe will have to agree to more and more concessions in order to save jobs and keep the labor movement going," he said. "They are not in a good situation either."

Indeed, union membership has also steadily fallen in Europe and the UK—and their support amongst the general population is not as high as it used to be.

Professor Justin Fisher, a political analyst at London's Brunel University, was quoted as saying that "the [British] unions have got to be careful in terms of getting public sympathy and the world has certainly changed in that respect."

Regarding the ability of UK unions to stop the British government's austerity program, Fisher states, "I don't think they can do anything about it. The days when the unions could hold the government to ransom in any serious and long-term way are behind us—but that's not to say there couldn't be some incredibly serious disruption."

EVALUATING THE AUTHOR'S ARGUMENTS:

In this viewpoint Palash R. Ghosh claims that unions have grown both less influential and more unpopular. Name at least one author in this chapter who takes an opposing view to Ghosh and one who agrees with him. Explain the precise way in which they agree or disagree.

Chapter 2

Should Government Regulate Labor Unions?

In 2010 Wisconsin's newly elected governor Scott Walker (pictured) speaks about his proposal to strip public-employee unions of their collective bargaining rights. The move caused a political firestorm in Wisconsin and sparked a contentious national debate.

Viewpoint

1

States Should Repeal Collective Bargaining in the Public Sector

Chris Edwards

"State governments should repeal collective bargaining in the public sector."

In the following viewpoint Chris Edwards argues that states should not allow collective bargaining by unions in the public sector. He contends that states that allow or mandate collective bargaining of public-sector employees end up paying much higher wages and benefits, which is causing shortfalls for state budgets. Although Edwards concedes that public-sector employees have the right to be in a union to voice their opinion about public policy, he denies that they have a right to collective bargaining. Edwards is the director of tax policy studies at the libertarian think tank the Cato Institute and the author of *Downsizing the Federal Government*.

AS YOU READ, CONSIDER THE FOLLOWING QUESTIONS:

1. According to Edwards, what percentage of state and local workers were members of unions in 2010?
2. Unionized public-sector workers earn a wage premium of about what percent over nonunionized public-sector workers, according to the author?
3. Edwards claims that collective bargaining is inconsistent with what freedom?

C haos in government. Tens of thousands of angry protesters in the streets. Schools closed. Yes, Wisconsin looks a lot like Egypt this week [February 14–18, 2011]. But while Arabs are fighting to end extraordinary overreach by government, Wisconsin union protesters are fighting to preserve it.

Collective Bargaining in the Public Sector

At the heart of the dispute is a bold plan by Wisconsin Gov. Scott Walker (R) to curtail collective bargaining by most but not all of his state's public-sector workers, including teachers. That is a long overdue reform—but the governor's plan doesn't go far enough! A dozen or so states, including Virginia, where I live, do not allow collective bargaining in the public sector at all, and these states are doing just fine without it.

The government union issue is coming to the forefront because states, facing huge deficits, are desperate to reform their budgets and cut pensions. Wisconsin is just one of several states where legislatures, empowered by Republican victories [in the November 2010 elections], are finally tackling one of the root causes: the ability of public-sector unions to squeeze taxpayers

> **FAST FACT**
>
> Collective bargaining consists of negotiations between an employer and a group of employees, usually through representation by a union, to set the conditions of employment.

for exorbitant benefits. In states that have unionized workforces, needed reforms are facing huge and aggressive anti-reform lobbying campaigns by the unions.

In 2010, 36 percent of state and local workers were members of unions, which is five times the union share in the US private sector. Yet prior to the 1960s, unions represented less than 15 percent of the state and local workforce. At the time, courts generally held that public-sector workers did not have the same union privileges that private workers had under the 1935 Wagner Act, such as collective bargaining.

A Boilermakers Union member at a plant in Wisconsin asks Governor Scott Walker if he expects political support from the Boilermakers after he strips away the collective bargaining rights of public-sector employees.

That changed during the 1960s and 1970s, as a flood of pro-union laws in dozens of states triggered a dramatic rise in public-sector unionism. Many states passed laws that encouraged collective bargaining in the public sector, as well as laws that imposed compulsory union dues.

Today, the union shares in government workforces vary widely by state. About 26 states have collective bargaining for essentially all state and local workers. A further 12 or so states have collective bargaining for a portion of their state and local workers, and the remaining 12 states do not have public sector collective bargaining. At the same time, 22 states have "right-to-work" laws, which free workers from being forced to join a union or pay union dues.

The Cost of Public Sector Unions

These differences in unionization between the states affect fiscal policy. Statistical studies find that unionized public sector workers earn a wage premium of about 10 percent over non-unionized public sector workers. This is important because employee compensation represents half of all state and local government spending.

Aside from inflated wages, public sector unions have pushed for excessive pension benefit levels, which are creating a fiscal crisis for many governments. That's another reason unions are so angry in Wisconsin: Governor Walker is demanding that state workers carry more of the burden for their health and pension plans.

Defined benefit pension plans are available to about four-fifths of state and local workers but just one-fifth of private workers. And public sector plans are typically about twice as generous as remaining private plans. That generosity has led to a $3 trillion funding gap in public sector pensions. That gap will create a huge burden on future taxpayers unless benefits are cut, and unions often stand in the way of such reforms.

Unions increase government costs in other ways. They often protect poorly performing workers, and they usually push for larger staffing levels than required. Unions typically discourage the use of inexpensive volunteers in government activities, and they create a more bureaucratic and inefficient workplace.

Unionism seems to coincide with poor state government management. States with higher public sector union shares tend to have higher levels of government debt. And the states with higher union shares

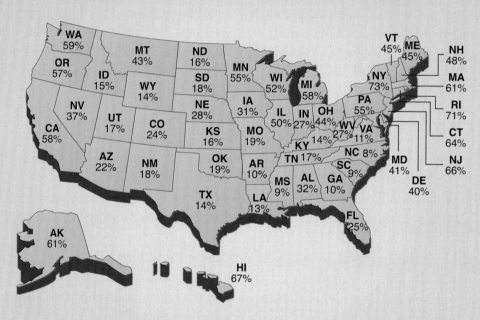

Union Shares of State and Local Government Employment

WA 59%
OR 57%
MT 43%
ND 16%
MN 55%
VT 45%
ME 45%
NH 48%
ID 15%
WY 14%
SD 18%
WI 52%
MI 58%
NY 73%
MA 61%
NV 37%
UT 17%
CO 24%
NE 28%
IA 31%
IL 50%
IN 27%
OH 44%
PA 55%
RI 71%
CA 58%
KS 16%
MO 19%
KY 14%
WV 27%
VA 11%
CT 64%
AZ 22%
NM 18%
OK 19%
AR 10%
TN 17%
NC 8%
SC 9%
MD 41%
NJ 66%
TX 14%
LA 13%
MS 9%
AL 32%
GA 10%
DE 40%
FL 25%
AK 61%
HI 67%

Taken from: Chris Edwards. "Public-Sector Unions." Tax & Budget Bulletin, no. 61, March 2010.

do more poorly on grading by the Pew Center regarding the quality of public sector management.

Inconsistent with Freedom of Association

Public sector unions are powerful special interest groups. The teachers unions, the American Federation of State, County, and Municipal Employees, and the Service Employees International Union have more than seven million members combined. They have well-financed political war chests and are very active in political campaigns.

Unions certainly have free speech rights to voice their opinions about public policy. But collective bargaining gives unions the exclusive right to speak for covered workers, many of whom may disagree with the views of the monopoly union. Thus, collective bargaining is inconsistent with the right to freedom of association.

In states such as Virginia, teachers and other government workers may form voluntary associations and lobby the government, which is fine. But collective bargaining—or monopoly unionism—gives a privileged position in our democracy to government insiders who focus on expanding the public sector to their own personal benefit.

Wisconsin's proposed union reforms are on the right track. But state governments should repeal collective bargaining in the public sector altogether, following the successful policies of Virginia, North Carolina, and other states. That would give policymakers the flexibility they need to make tough budget decisions on pensions and other fiscal challenges facing their states.

EVALUATING THE AUTHOR'S ARGUMENTS:

In this viewpoint Chris Edwards argues that public-sector employees do not have the same right to collective bargaining as private-sector employees. In what way does Garrett Keizer, author of the following viewpoint, dispute this claim? Whose argument do you find more convincing? Why?

Collective Bargaining Is a Right in Both the Private and Public Sectors

"Collective bargaining is an inheritance and we are all named in the will."

Garrett Keizer

In the following viewpoint Garrett Keizer argues that there is no important distinction to be made between private-sector and public-sector workers with respect to collective bargaining. All workers, he contends, have the right to bargain collectively. Furthermore, Keizer claims that the argument that the public sector is not for profit and is therefore different than the private sector is flawed. Keizer reasons that all jobs are subject to the attempts of management to profit from labor and so collective bargaining is needed to keep the profit margin reasonable for workers. Keizer is a contributing editor for *Harper's Magazine*, a writer, and a lecturer.

AS YOU READ, CONSIDER THE FOLLOWING QUESTIONS:
  1. According to Keizer, in what way do proponents of the two-labors theory say that private-sector and public-sector workers are different?
  2. Keizer contends that our entire economic system rests on what principle?
  3. What model for managing salaries, proposed by George Orwell, does the author endorse?

A s New Jersey throws its weight behind Wisconsin and Ohio in rolling back the collective bargaining rights of public sector employees, we are once again going to hear the argument that public sector unions ought not to be confused with their private sector counterparts. They're two different animals entirely.

The Two-Labors Fallacy

Private sector workers, so the argument goes, have historically organized to win better working conditions and a bigger piece of the pie from profit-making entities like railroads and coal mines. But public sector employees work for "us," the ultimate nonprofit, and therefore are not entitled to the same protections.

FAST FACT

According to the American Federation of Labor and Congress of Industrial Organizations, the average salary for a chief executive officer in 2010 was $11.4 million.

This is a fond notion at best. Yes, public school teachers were never gunned down by Pinkerton guards; municipal firefighters were never housed in company-owned shanties by the side of the tracks. But none of this cancels their rights as organized workers. No ancestor of mine voted to ratify the Constitution, either, but I have the same claim on the Bill of Rights as any Daughter of the American Revolution. Collective bargaining is an inheritance and we are all named in the will.

In Miami, Florida, private-sector union members march in solidarity with police officers and their supporters. Police are demanding a contract that is comparable to those of other major police departments in Florida.

The two-labors fallacy rests on an even shakier proposition: that profits exist only where there is an accountant to tally them. This is economics reduced to the code of a shoplifter—whatever the security guard doesn't see the store won't miss. If my wife and I have young children but are still able to enjoy the double-income advantages of a childless couple, isn't that partly because our children are being watched at school? If I needn't invest some of my household's savings in elaborate surveillance systems, isn't that partly because I have a patrol car circling the block? The so-called "public sector" is a profit-making entity; it profits me.

The Profit Margin

Denying this profitability has an obvious appeal to conservatives. It allows a union-busting agenda to hide behind nice distinctions. "We're not anti-union, we're just against certain kinds of unions." But the denial isn't exclusive to conservatives; in fact, it informs the delusional innocence of many liberals. I mean the idea that exploitation is the exclusive province of oil tycoons and other wicked types. If you own a yoga center or direct an M.F.A. [Master of Fine Arts] program, you can't possibly be implicated in the more scandalous aspects of capitalism—just as you can't possibly be to blame for racism if you've never grown cotton or owned a slave.

The fact is that our entire economic system rests on the principle of paying someone less than his or her labor is worth. The principle applies in the public sector no less than the private. The purpose of most labor unions has never been to eliminate the profit margin (the tragedy of the American labor movement) but rather to keep it within reasonable bounds.

But what about those school superintendents and police chiefs with their fabulous pensions, with salaries and benefits far beyond the average worker's dreams?

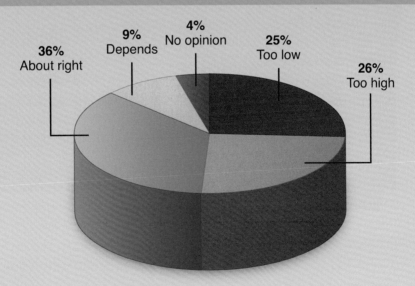

Americans' Views on Public-Sector Compensation

Do you think the salaries and benefits of most public employees are too high, too low, or about right for the work that they do?

36%
About right

9%
Depends

4%
No opinion

25%
Too low

26%
Too high

Taken from: *New York Times*/CBS News Poll, February 24–27, 2011.

Salaries in the Public and Private Sectors

Tell me about it. This past school year, I worked as a public high school teacher in northeastern Vermont. At 58 years of age, with a master's degree and 16 years of teaching experience, I earned less than $50,000. By the standards of the Ohio school superintendent or the Wisconsin police chief, my pension can only be described as pitiful, though the dairy farmer who lives down the road from me would be happy to have it.

He should have it, at the least, and he could. If fiscal conservatives truly want to "bring salaries into line" they should commit to a model similar to the one proposed by [English author] George Orwell 70 years ago, with the nation's highest income exceeding the lowest by no more than a factor of 10. They should establish that model in the public sector and enforce it with equal rigor and truly progressive taxation in the private.

Right now C.E.O.'s of multinational corporations earn salaries as much as a thousand times those of their lowest-paid employees. In such a context complaining about "lavish" public sector salaries is like shushing the foul language of children playing near the set of a snuff film. Whom are we kidding? More to the point, who's getting snuffed?

EVALUATING THE AUTHOR'S ARGUMENTS:

In this viewpoint Garrett Keizer argues that there is no significant difference between private-sector and public-sector workers affecting their right to use collective bargaining. What is a point of difference raised by Chris Edwards, author of the previous viewpoint, that Keizer does not address? What do you think Keizer would say about this difference?

Viewpoint
3

Right-to-Work Laws Protect Workers from Forced Unionization

"If a state has no right to work law, employers must negotiate with the union instead of the individual worker."

Bruce Walker

In the following viewpoint Bruce Walker argues that all labor unions today are coerced unions, except in right-to-work states, because employees are forced to join a union as a condition of employment in certain jobs. Walker contends that laws denying freedom in employment do not make life better, even if the unions promise otherwise. He concludes that labor unions are the enemies of liberty and calls for the end of forced unionization. Walker is an author and writes for *American Thinker.*

AS YOU READ, CONSIDER THE FOLLOWING QUESTIONS:

1. According to Walker, how many states have right-to-work laws?
2. The author claims that labor negotiations, rather than making an economic argument, have become exercises in what?
3. Walker claims that unions, especially for public employees, can function only in what kind of universe?

W here would we be without labor unions? We would be much better off.

Americans do not understand what "labor unions" mean. Nothing prevents a group of workers at a plant or office from getting together, signing an agreement which delegates power to negotiate contracts to certain representatives, and then proceeding with collective bargaining by those workers who chose to sign the agreement. That is not unionism; it is simply a business arrangement, much like when an athlete has an agent or a client has a lawyer.

The problem with unionism is that those who do not feel such an agreement is needed are compelled to surrender their right to bargain for their working conditions and compelled, as well, to support a vast, expensive bureaucracy of labor satraps [subordinate officials]. It is coercion of workers masked as industrial democracy. If 49% of the "represented" workers want a wage freeze but more vacation time, and that is not the official union position, then the union bosses are working against the interest of these workers. If many workers feel union rules reduce efficiency, and so the prospects of more jobs, those workers have to pay for the privilege of their representatives doing exactly the opposite of what they wish.

Coerced unions were always unnecessary, wasteful, and immoral —and all unions today are coerced unions. Depending upon whether a state has a "closed shop" (only members of a union can be hired, and these must comply with union rules) or "union shop" (new employees must join the union after being hired), if a state has no right to work law, employers must negotiate with the union instead of the individual worker. Only 22 states now have right to work laws, although robust Republican state governments could add six more states to that column, five in the Great Lakes region alone.

Through mostly Republican-controlled state legislatures, twenty-two states have passed right-to-work laws. Republicans have also targeted the five states in the Great Lakes region as needing to enact right-to-work legislation.

The Impact of Unions

Our Great Lakes Region was once the industrial dynamo of the world. Unions murdered its prosperity. Towns and cities in the Great Lakes that ought to be humming with activity are now dwindling into ghost towns.

People invariably can be persuaded that in free economic transactions, like the decision of people to work in a coalmine or tractor factory, the workers are getting the short end of the stick. Market economics, however, prevents "exploitation" from being more than a brief aberration and these fluctuations are as likely to unjustly enrich workers (for a short time) as to enrich employers. Only a mind focused on envy and anger can pretend that laws denying the liberty of employment somehow make life better.

It is blindingly clear to any open mind that unions, especially public employee unions, do not even pretend to make an economic argument for their position. Labor negotiations, more and more, are simply

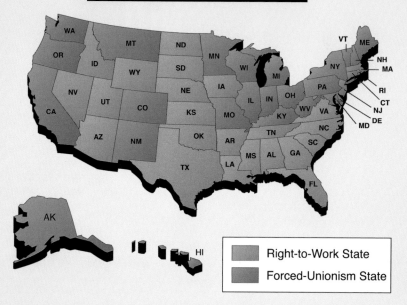

Right-to-Work States

Taken from: National Right to Work Legal Defense Foundation. www.nrtw.org.

exercises in naked political power. The dues snatched involuntarily from workers who oppose being drafted into supporting collectivist Democrats are used to buy politicians. Aside from the crushing "tax" upon our nation's economy which union dues and union restrictions on liberty cost our nation, the social effect of a work environment smothered beneath big labor, big business, and big government squeezes most Americans into lonely atoms in the business of America.

The Enemies of Liberty

These leviathans are the antithesis of what our country needs to survive and to thrive in a world of instant communication, evolving technology, and global market price systems. Few, if any, people in history have been such rugged individualists as Americans. Our ability to innovate, to adapt quickly, to push unconventional approaches to their limits—all these have made us great, and in more than just wealth and power. Unions are the antipode of this supreme American virtue. Unions are the incarnation of the putrid body of [Communist theorist Karl] Marx and all his bitter disciples.

Unions, including especially public employee unions, function only in a grim universe of constant conflict and suspicion. They are close siblings of feminists who find transcendent grievance in the fact of gender. Unions find family with "civil rights" activists, whose wealth and power are dependent upon the hopelessness of black people. Unions are natural cousins of personal injury lawyers whose only commandment is "Do anything to win" or leftist politicians whose guiding principle is "Promise anything."

The America of 2011 is shackled with crippling chains—tax rates, particularly on capital gains; environmental regulations calculated to impoverish us into "green" living; goose-stepping media who sappily salute any sin of leftism; militant atheism masking as some sort of faux-Americanism; vast and awful pyramids of public debt and fathomless seas of future entitlements—and so much more. Do we want a bright future? Do we want our country back? Abolish forced unionism, beginning with government workers. Republicans are weak, far too weak, on this particular issue. Unions are not just the political enemy of Republicans; they are the ideological enemies of liberty. Republicans should heed the quip of President [Ronald] Reagan when his assistants warned that some of his policies were too extreme: "What are they going to do to me? Hang me from a higher tree?"

EVALUATING THE AUTHOR'S ARGUMENTS:

In this viewpoint Bruce Walker suggests that right-to-work laws are about protecting the rights of individual workers. In what way does Dean Baker, author of the following viewpoint, disagree with this?

Right-to-Work Laws Aim to Reduce the Bargaining Power of Workers

"Right-to-work laws . . . are about reducing the bargaining power of workers."

Dean Baker

In the following viewpoint Dean Baker argues that there is a misconception that right-to-work laws are meant to protect the individual worker. Baker claims that workers are never forced to join a union, as some believe. What right-to-work laws do, he contends, is allow workers to be represented by a union without having to pay for it. Baker says that right-to-work laws result in labor unions' losing power, and, hence, they weaken collective bargaining clout for workers. Baker is codirector of the Center for Economic and Policy Research in Washington, DC. He is the author of *Taking Economics Seriously.*

AS YOU READ, CONSIDER THE FOLLOWING QUESTIONS:
  1. According to Baker, right-to-work laws prohibit what kind of employment contract?
  2. Baker draws an analogy between right-to-work laws and what other kind of law?
  3. States with right-to-work laws differ from states without laws in what way, according to the author?

P art of Wisconsin Gov. Scott Walker's union-busting agenda is including a "right to work" rule for public-sector employees. Several other Republican governors are considering similar measures for both the public and private sectors. Insofar as they succeed, these right-to-work measures will seriously weaken the bargaining power of workers.

Right-to-Work Laws

"Right to work" is a great name from the standpoint of proponents, just like the term "death tax" is effective for opponents of the estate tax, but it has nothing to do with the issue at hand. It is widely believed that in the absence of right-to-work laws workers can be forced to join a union. This is not true. Workers at any workplace always have the option as to whether or not to join a union.

Right-to-work laws prohibit contracts that require that all the workers who benefit from union representation to pay for union representation. In states without right-to-work laws, unions often sign contracts that require that all the workers in a bargaining unit pay a representation fee to the union that represents the bargaining unit.

The logic is straightforward. When a union is recognized as representing a bargaining unit, it legally must represent every worker in that unit, whether or not a worker opts to join the union.

This means not only that nonmembers get the same wages and benefits that the union negotiates with the employer, but the union is also obligated to represent any nonmember individually if that worker gets in a dispute with the employer over an issue covered in the contract. For example, if a nonunion member is threatened with a discipline action or firing, the union must defend this worker's rights just the same as if they were in the union.

Right-to-work laws prohibit workers from being required to pay for this union representation. What right-to-work laws actually guarantee is the ability for a worker to benefit from union representation without having to pay for union representation.

An Analogy

Copyrights provide a good analogy to this situation. As we know, it costs money to produce recorded music or movies. All the people who take part in the productions, musicians, actors, technical assistants, and others need to be paid.

Copyright is a mechanism that allows these people to be paid for their work. (It is not the only mechanism for financing creative work, but it is currently the main mechanism for generating revenue for those involved in producing creative work.) Under copyright law, the holder of the copyright is given a monopoly over the distribution of the copyrighted material. The copyright holder can sue for damages anyone who distributes or uses copyrighted material without their permission.

"Wisconsin's War on Unions," Cartoon by Keith Tucker. www.CartoonStock.com.

If we applied the logic of right-to-work laws to copyright, then copyright holders would be prohibited from taking steps to enforce their copyright. If people chose, they could pay the copyright protected price for music or movies, but they would also have the option to freely download copyright protected material without paying the copyright holder. And there would be nothing the copyright holder could do.

This would be the parallel of "right to work" in the copyright world. As it stands, copyright holders are having a difficult time enforcing their copyrights and getting paid for their work (which might suggest a more modern mechanism for financing creative work would be desirable), but imagine that copyright holders had no legal recourse.

> **FAST FACT**
>
> A study by the Economic Policy Institute found that in states with right-to-work laws only 7.6 percent of workers are represented by a union, compared with 18.6 percent in states without such laws.

It is unlikely that many people would choose to pay for the music they listened to or the movies that they watched if there was nothing stopping them from enjoying this material without paying. This is the situation in which right-to-work laws put unions.

The Real Goal of Right-to-Work Laws

The outcome is obvious; unions will have a much more difficult time staying in place, as many workers will take advantage of the opportunity to get all the benefits of union representation without paying for them. The unions that do survive will be much weaker if the government forces the union to represent people who don't have to pay for its services.

This is why the states with right-to-work laws have much lower rates of union representation than states without such laws. If the government rigs the deck against unions, then it will be very hard for them to survive, just as it would be hard to sell copyrighted material in a world where copyrights were altogether unenforceable.

Even without right-to-work laws, any worker always has the right to not join a union. If they dislike the union enough, they have the option to work somewhere else, just as they would do if they disliked the employer enough. Of course, workers also can vote out bad union leaders or vote to get rid of the union altogether as well, options that they do not have vis-à-vis their employer.

In short, right-to-work laws have nothing to do with protecting the rights of individual workers. They are about reducing the bargaining power of workers: pure and simple.

Union members cast votes for their leadership. It is widely believed that in the absence of right-to-work laws, workers can be forced to join a union. However, according to the author, employees at any workplace have the option to join a union.

The Employee Free Choice Act Should Be Passed

AFL-CIO

"America needs to restore the freedom for all of its workers to bargain for a better life by passing the Employee Free Choice Act."

In the following viewpoint the AFL-CIO (American Federation of Labor and Congress of Industrial Organizations) argues that the Employee Free Choice Act would help restore the freedom of workers to join unions, improving life for all Americans. The AFL-CIO contends that the law protecting workers' rights to collective bargaining has been weakened over the decades, resulting in deunionization. The AFL-CIO claims that increased unionization would increase productivity, decrease income inequality, and improve the economy. The AFL-CIO is a voluntary federation of fifty-six national and international labor unions representing over 12 million workers.

AS YOU READ, CONSIDER THE FOLLOWING QUESTIONS:
  1. What percentage of US workers say they want a union in their workplace, according to a study cited by the author?
  2. During what two decades in American history was union membership at its highest, according to the AFL-CIO?
  3. According to the author, what impact does union membership have on voter participation?

A merica cannot be a successful low-wage consumer society. The [George W.] Bush administration tried to make up for stagnant wages with consumer debt—a choice that has proven disastrous. Our country needs more money to go to America's workers and less to Wall Street speculators and CEOs. That is why a key element of our nation's economic recovery must be to restore workers' freedom to form unions, speak for themselves and negotiate a fair share of the wealth they create. Rising income, not more debt, is the only way out of the economic crisis.

The Deunionization of America

America became the greatest middle class society in the world when our country respected workers' fundamental human right to represent themselves and bargain for better wages and benefits. Through bargaining, workers transform bad, dead-end jobs into living-wage jobs with opportunities for training and upgrading. The long-term decline in collective bargaining coverage is a significant cause not only of wage stagnation but also of the nation's health care and retirement income security crises—crises that grow worse by the day.

But the law that protects workers' freedom to bargain has been perverted. Companies routinely fire workers who stand up for themselves. Workers who want to form unions are threatened with plant closings, interrogated, offered bribes, spied on and intimidated. The result? Only 8 percent of private-sector workers actually belong to unions, even though independent surveys by a leading national survey firm show that 58 percent of U.S. workers say they want a union in their workplace—the highest percentage in 25 years.

Denying Americans the freedom to form unions at their place of work is not just unfair, it is destructive economic policy. Taking away workers' rights on the job has hurt the American middle class, increased economic inequality and destabilized our economy. With deunionization, we have set off a long-term downward spiral of lower wages and fewer benefits. Pockets of workers with good jobs try to hold on to a middle class standard of living, even as more and more people suffer lower wages, less health care and no retirement security. As companies fight to cut costs, consumer demand falls, breeding recession and instability.

Unions and Productivity

Over the past 35 years, workers' productivity has risen by more than 75 percent, but inflation-adjusted wages of America's workers—as published by the President's Council of Economic Advisors [in 2008]—are lower than in 1973. The reality today for America's workers is:

1. Stagnant wages and rising economic inequality.
2. Pessimism and deepening worker dissatisfaction with their economic prospects.

A multitude of published studies by respected and prominent economists have found that when workers have the right to come together and form unions, their lives improve and the larger economy is healthier: Productivity rises, product and service quality improves, economic inequality is reduced and wages are boosted substantially for all workers—but especially for low-wage workers and workers of color. Unions and collective bargaining have been especially important in giving workers access to health insurance and defined-benefit pensions.

FAST FACT

According to the US Census Bureau, the median income for men in 2010 was $32,137 compared with a median income in 1973 of $35,336 (in 2010 dollars).

During the 1950s and 1960s, when America's economy grew at the fastest rate since World War II, the percentage of workers who had unions was at its highest point in

American Opinion on the Employee Free Choice Act

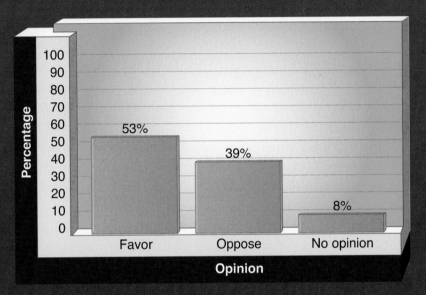

Generally speaking, would you favor or oppose a new law that would make it easier for labor unions to organize workers?

Taken from: Gallup Poll, March 14–15, 2009.

U.S. history. Conversely, on the eve of the worst economic crisis of the 20th century, the Great Depression, union membership had been declining for more than a decade, just as it is today. The times in our history when workers have been able to come together to speak for themselves in the workplace have been times of rising real wages, economic and financial stability, rising health care coverage, rising pension coverage and rising productivity. But when workers' rights are repressed, the American economy produces gross inequality and financial instability.

Some responsible and profitable major corporations have adopted majority sign-up as standard practice and an important element of their corporations' successful high-road business plans. The result for companies like AT&T and Kaiser Permanente has been workplaces with better labor-management relations, less tension, more respect for employees and a positive impact on employee morale.

The Positive Impact of Unions

Of course, there are employers that want America to be a low-wage economy. The U.S. Chamber of Commerce has issued white papers attacking workers' freedom to organize, relying on writings by a handful of far right-wing economists.

What the Chamber doesn't want policymakers to know is that union membership is the route out of poverty for workers in low-wage occupations. For example, union cashiers earn 30 percent more than nonunion cashiers, union dining room and cafeteria attendants earn 49 percent more than nonunion dining room and cafeteria attendants, and union janitors earn 31 percent more than nonunion janitors.

Today, states with the highest union density enjoy higher wages, higher family incomes, lower poverty rates and smaller percentages of people without health insurance than states with the lowest union density.

When workers can form unions, rising wages set off a positive, upward cycle. States with the highest union density spend more per pupil on public education; pay teachers higher salaries; have more doctors per capita, lower infant mortality and lower death rates; have a lower incidence of workplace fatalities; and have better worker safety net programs such as unemployment insurance and workers' compensation than states with the lowest union density. Unions not only improve the quality of worker protection programs at state and federal levels—they inform and educate workers about these programs and help them gain access to their benefits and protections.

Unions also have a large positive impact on civic participation by America's workers. It comes as no surprise that the states with the highest union density have higher voter participation rates than states with the lowest union density.

The Employee Free Choice Act

Unions and collective bargaining are vital not only in the workplace but also in society at large. Half a century ago, the groundbreaking economist John Kenneth Galbraith identified unions as a vital source of countervailing power in an economy dominated by large corporations. That remains true today.

The Employee Free Choice Act is part of a strategy for American economic revival—for a high-wage, high-skill economy. Increasing incomes and respecting workers' rights on the job must be a central part of that strategy.

What is the plan proposed by the anti-worker voices in the business community? More consumer debt? More subprime mortgages?

In a March 2009 press conference, Iowa senator Tom Harkin (right) and California representative George Miller announce the introduction of the Employee Free Choice Act aimed at restoring American rights in the workplace.

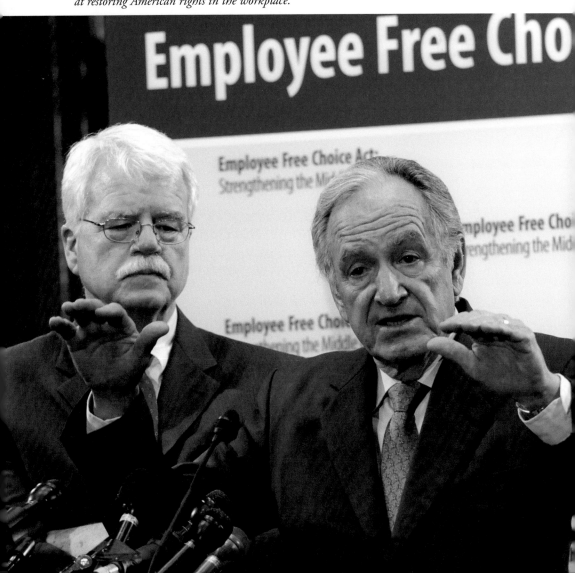

More jobs without pensions and health care? A vain effort to compete with low-wage countries by cutting our standard of living to their levels for all but the wealthiest Americans?

America deserves better than economic inequality and economic decline. That's why America needs to restore the freedom for all of its workers to bargain for a better life by passing the Employee Free Choice Act.

EVALUATING THE AUTHOR'S ARGUMENTS:

In this viewpoint the AFL-CIO claims that the majority of workers want to belong to a union. What statistic does Doug Bandow, author of the following viewpoint, cite as evidence that workers want no such thing? Explain how it is possible for both statistics to be true.

Viewpoint 6

The Employee Free Choice Act Should Not Be Passed

Doug Bandow

"Congress should say no to big labor's push for the Employee Free Choice Act."

In the following viewpoint Doug Bandow argues that Congress should resist the pressure from union leaders to pass the Employee Free Choice Act. Bandow contends that organized labor wants to pass the law because Americans are largely rejecting unions. He claims that the current law protects employees' rights by allowing secret-ballot elections for union recognition, whereas the Employee Free Choice Act would allow unions to intimidate workers into joining a union without an election and without secret ballots. Bandow is a senior fellow at the libertarian think tank the Cato Institute who specializes in foreign policy and civil liberties issues.

AS YOU READ, CONSIDER THE FOLLOWING QUESTIONS:
1. According to the author, unions lose what percentage of organizing elections?
2. Bandow claims that the Employee Free Choice Act would have the unfortunate effects of rewarding unions' misrepresentation and intimidation and what other effect?
3. The employees of how many companies rejected union representation in January 2009, according to Bandow?

O rganized labor is on the march, with Democrats in control of both ends of Pennsylvania Avenue. The top priority for big labor has been the Employee Free Choice Act; it may not be possible to pass the bill this session [spring 2009], but unions continue to push for it. Even a small electoral change in 2010 could put the issue back in play.

Americans' Rejection of Unions

Organizers want Congress to help them intimidate their way to victory, because, as it is, too many workers are saying no to unions. Today just 7.6 percent of private-sector workers belong to unions. Only in government employment has unions' representation been growing. Most Americans recognize that they will have more opportunity in a vibrant, growing economy than in the sort of calcified system favored by labor-union executives. This has long been the case: Even in organized labor's glory years, it never played the leading political role in the U.S. that it achieved in Europe. The American economy always was more open and entrepreneurial.

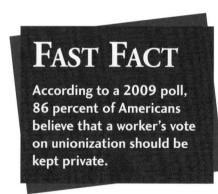

FAST FACT

According to a 2009 poll, 86 percent of Americans believe that a worker's vote on unionization should be kept private.

But union activists don't get it. In organized labor's view, if employees vote no—unions lose 40 percent of organizing elections—it must

There is a bill in Congress called the Employee Free Choice Act that would effectively replace a federally supervised secret-ballot election with a process that requires a majority of workers to simply sign a card to authorize organizing a union and the workers' signatures would be made public to their employer, the union organizers, and their coworkers. Do you support or oppose Congress passing this legislation?

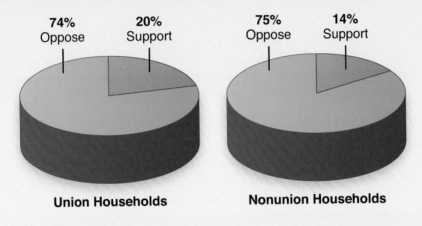

74% Oppose   20% Support   75% Oppose   14% Support

Union Households   **Nonunion Households**

Taken from: McLaughlin & Associates. "American Voters Reject the Employee Free Choice Act," January 2009.

be a result of corporate perfidy. If you listen to the rhetoric of big-labor executives, you would think that American unions were battling Adolf Hitler's Germany or Joseph Stalin's Soviet Union on behalf of human rights and individual liberty. For instance, the AFL-CIO [American Federation of Labor and Congress of Industrial Organizations] declared that in America "workers still lack the freedom to form unions." Apparently labor organizers are being hauled off in handcuffs, and workers are being tossed into the Gulag [a Soviet prison camp].

The Employee Free Choice Act

To stop employees from saying no so often, unions have proposed to rig the system: Under the Employee Free Choice Act, whenever a union gets more than half of a company's workers to sign unionization cards—in a process known as "card check"—the National Labor Relations Board [NLRB] can certify the union right then and there, without an election. Such a process would have two unfortunate effects.

The first would be to reward unions' misrepresentation and intimidation. Workers across America testify that union organizers use all manner of techniques in pressuring workers to sign, and that they regularly deceive employees about the impact of signing a card (as the law stands today, the NLRB can certify a union based on card check, but only if the employer agrees). Also, card check makes employees' views on unionization public. Relying on signed cards in lieu of a secret-ballot election is akin to a poll in the Soviet Union, where you showed your ballot to the local political commissar before dropping it into the box.

Second, card check would simplify the unpleasant—for organized labor—process of persuading workers that they would get a better deal by joining a union. An organizing campaign allows the company

Senate minority leader Mitch McConnell (pictured) speaks in opposition to the Employee Free Choice Act. Opinions on the law have highlighted the marked differences between the two parties, with Democrats supporting the act and Republicans against it.

as well as the union to make its case. One reason we don't choose the president of the United States by collecting signed cards is that we believe that an election campaign, however flawed, helps develop issues and answer questions. If the union's argument is a good one, organizers shouldn't fear a vote in which the company can politick as well.

Efforts to Defeat Unions

Unions support the Employee Free Choice Act not out of principle, but out of concern for their own success. In fact, labor officials like elections—when workers are seeking to toss out a union. Citing a U.S. Supreme Court case, the AFL-CIO shamelessly contended: The "representation election system provides the surest means of avoiding decisions which are 'the result of group pressures and not individual decision.'" No card check here: If you want to decertify a union, you have to defeat it in a secret ballot.

Still, many efforts to defeat unions succeed. Although the number of organizing elections has been falling in recent years, the number of decertification elections has remained relatively constant over the last decade, at more than 300 annually. While unions have pushed up their win ratio from 50 to 60 percent in certification votes (though participating in fewer elections), they have been consistently *losing* 60 to 70 percent of decertification ballots.

The NLRB's records show the extent and breadth of worker dissatisfaction with unions. In its six-month report filed last September [2008], the NLRB reported that unions lost 78 of 141 decertification elections. In the prior six-month period, unions lost 86 of 149 votes. And in January 2009 alone, unions lost their representation power over the employees of eight companies ranging from the Cradle of Aviation Museum in New York to the Chariton Valley Electric Cooperative in Iowa to the Crystal Care Center in Minnesota. In eight more companies, decertification elections were held, but the unions held on to power.

The Current Law

Workers, not employers, initiated all these votes. Obviously, even though employees often believe a union's initial sales pitch, many workers come to realize that the union option is not the right one.

And with a secret-ballot election available to protect them from intimidation and retaliation, they feel free to vote their consciences. As a result, unions lose more often than not.

Labor law is an inefficient mishmash. Instead of micro-managing business-labor relations, government's principal responsibilities should be to enforce contracts, prevent intimidation, and punish violence. But having set up a regulatory structure to promote unionization, Washington has a responsibility to protect workers as they express their preferences. And that requires preserving secret-ballot elections for union recognition.

That unions take the opposite position should come as no surprise. Contrary to the impression created by the white-hot rhetoric of union executives, American workers are not prevented from organizing. In fact, current law guarantees genuine "free choice" for employees by preserving their right to a secret ballot—precisely the problem in the view of labor executives, who want more money and influence. Congress should say no to big labor's push for the Employee Free Choice Act.

EVALUATING THE AUTHOR'S ARGUMENTS:

In this viewpoint Doug Bandow denies that the Employee Free Choice Act protects free choice. Considering the other viewpoints in this chapter, who do you think would agree with Bandow and who would disagree? Why?

Chapter 3

What Is the Future of Labor Unions?

Union issues came to the forefront of public awareness in 2011, when large protests against an antiunion bill affecting public employees in Wisconsin quickly spread to other states. Here, government workers in New York City rally in support of the Wisconsin protesters.

A Political War Is Being Waged to Eliminate Labor Unions

"It isn't as if these types of attacks on unions are new; what's different is their scale, intensity and real possibility of success."

Jane McAlevey

In the following viewpoint Jane McAlevey argues that there is an ongoing assault on labor unions that has escalated in recent years and has been successful in weakening unions. She contends that a variety of legislation has passed or is under way to weaken unions. McAlevey claims that there has been an upsurge in attempts to limit the power of unions in the public sector and a push for more privatization. She warns that the current campaign against unions is threatening to erase gains made for workers by unions in the past. McAlevey is a union and community organizer, educator, and author.

AS YOU READ, CONSIDER THE FOLLOWING QUESTIONS:

1. According to the author, how many states have right-to-work legislation and how many others have filed for it?
2. Corporations outspent unions in the November 2010 election by what factor, according to McAlevey?
3. According to McAlevey, what was the unionization rate in the private sector in 1975?

Emboldened by November's [2010] election results, corporations and their right-wing allies have launched what they hope will be their final offensive against America's unions. Their immediate target is government workers' unions. While New Jersey's Republican Governor Chris Christie has gained national fame by beating up on public school teachers, the threat to unionized workers is playing out in all fifty states, to the drumbeat in the media about states going broke because of government workers' wages, pensions and benefits. By late January [2011], with the swearing-in ceremonies complete in the twenty-one states where Republicans have a "trifecta," controlling the governor's office and both statehouses, hundreds of bills had been introduced seeking to hem in unions if not ban them altogether. On February 11, Wisconsin's new Republican Governor Scott Walker made what amounts to a declaration of all-out war on public sector workers in his historically progressive state, moving to deprive them of the very right to bargain collectively on matters essential to their economic security.

New Jersey Republican governor Chris Christie (pictured) has been an outspoken opponent of public-employee unions. The author says that the rights of employees in the public sector are being legislated against in states controlled by Republicans.

Legislation Attacking Unions

Walker's gambit has rightly elicited outrage, but considering the breadth of the attack unions are facing nationally, it is only the tip of the iceberg. Right-to-work legislation has been filed in twelve states; this is in addition to the twenty-two that already have such laws on the books. In technical terms, this legislation makes it illegal for employers to condition employment on union membership or the equivalent dues payments even when a majority of workers vote to form a union; practically speaking, it makes building and maintaining a strong union very difficult, which in turn makes it harder to organize new workplaces because there are few positive examples of unions to point to. In Virginia, the corporations and right-wing ideologues decided that the existing right-to-work law wasn't sufficient, and introduced a measure to embed the right-to-work provisions in the state Constitution. Three more states—Montana, Ohio and Wisconsin—are expected to have bills introduced converting their legal status to right-to-work.

Alabama passed legislation in January that bans public employee unions from collecting dues unless the unions first prove that none of the money will be used for supporting election campaigns. In every

"Labor Day Color." Copyright © by R.J. Matson and CagleCartoons.com. All rights reserved.

subsequent year after the initial certification, the union must submit itemized reports accounting for how its money is being spent. This law, sold as "paycheck protection" by the right but known as "paycheck deception" among union activists, has been introduced in four other states this year, including Arizona, Kansas, Mississippi and Missouri. In California there has already been ballot initiative language submitted to do the same. Using a variety of legal tools, these measures prohibit the use of union dues for political activity. Union advocates are expecting twelve more states to file bills or initiatives banning the collection of union monies for politics.

Building and construction unions are facing their own daunting line-up of bills that would gut prevailing wage laws and what are known as Project Labor Agreements (PLAs). These measures facilitate collective bargaining and the division of labor for unionized construction jobs, particularly construction jobs with public financing. In twenty states there is legislation expected to ban PLAs. In Iowa the new governor, Terry Branstad, was so excited to take up the challenge, he undid PLAs with his first executive order. The new governor of Ohio, John Kasich, has pledged to eliminate prevailing wage laws. It's hard to say whether Missouri or Maine will beat him to his goal, though: Missouri's legislation to ban prevailing wages has been introduced, and the new governor of Maine appointed the head of the building and construction industry organization to the position of state legislative director, a sure sign that he's serious about eliminating such laws. The AFL-CIO [American Federation of Labor and Congress of Industrial Organizations] says it anticipates anti–prevailing wage laws in fifteen states.

The Attack on Public Sector Workers

It is government workers, however, who face attacks in every state. Teacher tenure is being targeted in five states: New Jersey, Nevada, Indiana, Idaho and Florida. Laws that would allow parents, by petition, to "trigger" an entire school district to move to charter schools or to voucher programs are expected in at least eleven states. States that are considering either weakening or removing entirely the ability of public sector workers to bargain collectively include not only Wisconsin but Ohio, South Dakota, Colorado, Michigan, Nebraska, New Hampshire and Oklahoma. Measures to dismantle benefits for government workers are expected in some form in all fifty states. [Former House Speaker] Newt Gingrich and [former Florida governor] Jeb Bush, meanwhile, are pushing to allow states to declare bankruptcy, which would enable them to break their agreements that cover the pensions of hundreds of thousands of retired government workers. On top of all this, President [Barack] Obama has called for a freeze on federal workers' pay.

At the same time, a push to privatize public assets and services is mounting, posing a dire threat to public workers. Groups like In the Public Interest are working to hold back the privatization tide, but the momentum is on the other side. Donald Cohen, the group's chair, notes a recent shift in the nature of the opposition. "The entire world of public administration is being driven by a new cartel of consulting firms who offer their services to elected leaders—peddling themselves as efficiency experts," he says, explaining that these firms are increasingly playing the role that used to be filled by right-wing think tanks. "They are accounting firms, law firms and more who promote privatization, and they make money for completing the deal. And yet it has very little to do with efficiency and probably nothing to do with actually improving public services."

It isn't as if these types of attacks on unions are new; what's different is their scale, intensity and real possibility of success. After outspending unions in November's election by an estimated 4-to-1 margin, corporations and their allies are exploiting the fiscal crises across the nation to drive a stake into the heart of what is left of organized labor—public workers' unions. According to the just-released Bureau of Labor Statistics annual report for 2010, the overall union membership rate in America continued its slide, dropping from 12.3 percent to 11.9 percent. But perhaps most striking is the way unionization is skewed when comparing private sector workers, who are just 6.9 percent unionized, and public sector workers, 36.2 percent of whom belong to unions. The public sector, in other words, is labor's last stronghold.

An Ongoing Campaign to Weaken Unions

Grover Norquist laid out a sort of blueprint for the current right-wing assault in the February 2001 *American Spectator.* Identifying labor unions as the first of "five pillars" of Democratic strength, he calculated that they "raise $8 billion a year from 16 million union members paying an average of $500 dues," and outlined a game plan for destroying union power, key to the right's larger mission of abolishing all regulations that impede its agenda, from environmental laws to occupational safety to affirmative action.

But, of course, the right's campaign against labor has been decades in the making. In 1975 the overall unionization rate in the private sector was 25 percent. Thanks to the class war that has been waged since then—involving trade liberalization, radical reorganization of global finance rules, unionbusting, deindustrialization, rejiggered accounting rules and more—Norquist's goal is now within reach for the right. According to union expert and author Bill Fletcher Jr., "There has been a three-decade campaign by the neoliberal Democrats and the right wing to destroy the base of the strength of the American middle class, which can be boiled down to unions and government regulation of corporate excess. As a result, unionization rates and corresponding pay and benefits now appear higher in the government sector, and the same forces are now attacking government workers' unions."

FAST FACT

According to the US Bureau of Labor Statistics, the number of wage-earning and salaried workers belonging to unions declined by 612,000 between 2009 and 2010.

The irony, according to Janice Fine, professor at the Rutgers School of Management and Labor Relations, is that in the 1960s it was the private sector workers who earned more than their government counterparts. "Back then, the private sector unions helped the government workers get organized as part of a program to raise the standards for all workers," she notes. Now, as Ed Ott, former director of the New York City Central Labor Council, puts it, "After thirty years of wage suppression in the private sector, big business wants to compare wages and benefits between the private sector and the government sector." Republican presidential hopeful Tim Pawlenty did just that in a recent *Wall Street*

Journal op-ed. "Unionized public employees are making more money, receiving more generous benefits, and enjoying greater job security than the working families forced to pay for it with ever-higher taxes, deficits and debt," he wrote. These claims are distorted, but to the extent that public workers do enjoy hard-won union benefits, they have a target painted on their back.

EVALUATING THE AUTHOR'S ARGUMENTS:

In this viewpoint Jane McAlevey claims that Republicans are targeting labor unions. What is a possible explanation for why Republicans, rather than Democrats, are less supportive of labor unions?

Viewpoint

2

Labor Unions' Decline Is Due to Their Anticompetitive Nature

Daniel Griswold

"The main reason behind the decline of . . . labor unions in recent decades is the anti-competitive nature of unions them-selves.

In the following viewpoint Daniel Griswold argues that labor unions have been in decline in the last several decades because they destroy the competitiveness of businesses. Griswold claims that studies show that nonunionized companies do better than those that are unionized. Griswold contends that the reason there has been no decline in governmental unionization is because there is no competition. He concludes that workers are better off without unions and that government should resist implementing any legislation that would increase unionization, thereby harming businesses and workers. Griswold is director of the Herbert A. Stiefel Center for Trade Policy Studies at the Cato Institute, a libertarian Washington think tank.

AS YOU READ, CONSIDER THE FOLLOWING QUESTIONS:
1. What fraction of American workers belonged to unions fifty years ago, according to Griswold?
2. What does the author claim explains the job losses in manufacturing from 1973 through 2006 among unionized workers?
3. Since the early 1990s what fraction of new jobs has been in the service sectors, according to Griswold?

U.S. labor union leaders see themselves as champions of the American worker, but their movement has become largely irrelevant to most workers. . . . For the small and declining share of Americans who still work in unionized industries, the movement has proven to be a job killer.

The Reason for a Decline in Unions

From their zenith in the 1950s, labor unions have witnessed a relentless decline among non-governmental workers. Fifty years ago, about one in three Americans working in the private sector belonged to a labor union. Since then, "union density" in the private sector has declined steadily to less than 8 percent today.

Labor leaders blame the decline on union-busting corporations, years of hostile Republican rule in Washington, and a flood of imports from low-wage countries such as China, but the main reason behind the decline of private sector labor unions in recent decades is the anti-competitive nature of unions themselves. Like a virus, labor unions have been slowly sapping the lifeblood of the very industries and companies that employ their members.

Studies comparing unionized companies to those without unions find that unionized firms are less able to compete in the domestic or global marketplace. Unions can help raise productivity and reduce worker turnover, but at a steep cost to unionized employers. Through collective bargaining, unions extract higher above-market pay and benefits from employers, while more rigid union work rules reduce efficiency and blunt the ability of management to adapt to changing market conditions.

As a result, unions cripple the ability of the companies to compete in an open and dynamic economy. Research by Dr. Barry Hirsch at Georgia State University and others has found that unionized firms are less profitable, invest fewer resources in physical and intellectual capital, accumulate more debt, and grow more slowly than comparable firms that are not unionized.

The Damage Done by Unions

The inevitable outcome of the "union tax" is that unionized firms inevitably yield market share to their non-unionized rivals, whether foreign or domestic. The union tax explains why almost all the job losses in manufacturing from 1973 through 2006 were among unionized workers.

An obvious example of this phenomenon is the Big Three U.S. automakers. Since the 1970s, General Motors, Ford, and Chrysler

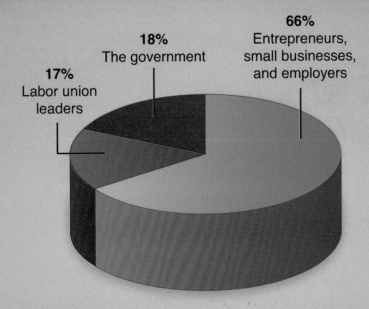

Union Members' Views on Job Growth

From the following list, whom do you trust most *to lead America to better job growth?*

17%
Labor union
leaders

18%
The government

66%
Entrepreneurs,
small businesses,
and employers

Taken from: Luntz Global Poll, October 2010.

have been losing ground to foreign-owned rivals such as Toyota, Honda, and Nissan.

It is not imports that have cut into the sales of the Big Three but output from foreign-owned plants in right-to-work states in the South such as Texas, Mississippi, Tennessee, Kentucky, and South Carolina.

Those non-unionized foreign "transplants" offer solid middle-class wages and benefits to their workers. They have managed to remain financially viable during the downturn because they avoided the gold-plated pay and benefit packages and stultifying work rules that the United Auto Workers union extracted from the Big Three over the years—contracts that proved to be unsustainable in a competitive market suffering through a steep recession.

Unionization has exacted a toll on other sectors of our economy as well. Many big city newspapers that have been hemorrhaging red ink are also unionized. The unionized airline industry has collectively lost billions of dollars in recent years.

The U.S. Postal Service is on track to lose $7 billion in the current fiscal year [2009] even though it enjoys a government-conferred monopoly on first-class mail. Of course, technology and the business cycle have done the most damage in those sectors, but the union tax seems to be the common thread among the most critically ill employers.

A new Toyota truck nears completion on an assembly line in Texas. Union opponents say that nonunion auto plants in the United States are more competitive than their unionized counterparts in Detroit.

Progress in the Non-Unionized Sector

The one sector where unions have managed to hold their ground is in government. Union density among government workers has held steady at between 33 and 36 percent of total public employment. Unions can survive and thrive in the government sector because, by definition, there is no real competition. The costs of unionization can be passed along to taxpayers without losing market share.

American workers do not need collective bargaining to enjoy the fruits of a free and open market. The Great Recession of 2007–09 has caused widespread pain, but

it should not be allowed to obscure the long-term progress American workers and their families have made in recent decades.

The real compensation per hour earned by American workers—that is, wages and benefits adjusted for inflation—is still 20 percent higher on average than a decade ago. Median household income is $6,000 higher than it was in the early 1990s. And despite the recent drop in home values and stock prices, median family net worth was still 10 percent higher in real dollars at the end of 2008 than a decade ago, and 30 percent higher than 20 years ago.

It remains one of the big lies of the economic debate that we have traded away high-paying, unionized manufacturing jobs for low-paying non-union service jobs flipping burgers and cashiering at a big-box retailer. Since the early 1990s, two-thirds of the net new jobs added to our economy have been in service sectors—such as education, health care, and business, financial and professional services—where average wages are higher than manufacturing. The American middle class today earns its keep in the largely non-unionized service sector.

The Danger of Further Unionization

The [Barack] Obama administration and Democratic congressional leaders owe a big political debt to the AFL-CIO [American Federation of Labor and Congress of Industrial Organizations], Teamsters and other labor organizations that expended so much money and manpower to get them elected. The so-far unsuccessful effort to pass "card check" legislation is just one example of the payback labor leaders expect to receive for their loyal backing.

Known officially as the Employee Free Choice Act, the card-check legislation would effectively abolish the secret ballot in workplace elections for union representation. It would also require employers to submit to binding government arbitration if they cannot reach an agreement with union representatives, forcing companies to submit to contracts that may imperil their very survival. And the bill would compress the time period for holding elections, denying workers the ability to fully inform themselves of the consequences of their decision.

Those are reasons enough to be wary of upsetting the current status quo in U.S. labor law. But the sobering experience of unionized companies offers a further warning against tipping the playing field further in favor of union organizers.

A resurgence of union representation in the private sector would threaten to plunge even more U.S. companies into financial distress and put more American workers in danger of losing their jobs.

> **EVALUATING THE AUTHOR'S ARGUMENTS:**
>
> In this viewpoint Daniel Griswold claims that unionized jobs have disappeared because unions cripple businesses. In what way might Jane McAlevey, author of the previous viewpoint, dispute this?

Viewpoint

3

America Needs Labor Unions to Counteract the Power of Big Business

David Macaray

"The only entity capable of taking on Big Business is Big Labor."

In the following viewpoint David Macaray argues that labor unions are vital to ensuring a good future for American workers. Macaray claims that the only way to neutralize the extensive power corporations wield in the United States is through unions. He claims that despite the arguments of those who say unions are not necessary anymore, unions are the only way to keep workers out of poverty and keep the gap between rich and poor in check. Macaray is a Los Angeles playwright, a former labor representative, and author of *It's Never Been Easy: Essays on Modern Labor.*

A s Detroit's multi-millionaire executives continue to mix it up with the struggling UAW [United Auto Workers], arguing over how to resuscitate a dying and woefully mismanaged industry without totally annihilating the wages and benefits the union spent 60 years fighting to get, the [Barack] Obama administration agonizes over what to do next.

Of the Big Three automakers, GM [General Motors] seems to be in the worst shape. In fact, on Feb. 14 [2009], it was leaked that GM plans to announce this week that unless it receives more federal loan guarantees (in addition to the $13 billion it already received), it will declare bankruptcy [GM ended up receiving almost $50 billion in federal assistance].

The Next Level for Labor Unions

When the conversation turns to the topic of unions, it's discouraging to hear people praise organized labor's historical role in reshaping American society—more or less "inventing" the middle-class—and then, in the same breath, declare that unions are, at best, anachronisms, or, at worst, unwieldy obstacles to economic progress.

Many of the same folks who glowingly acknowledge labor's contributions—equal pay for women, abolishing child labor, the 8-hour day, the 5-day week, overtime premiums, paid vacation, sick pay, pensions, maternity leave, mandatory safety programs, and company-paid health insurance—will sigh and announce that, alas, we don't really need unions any more.

Presumably, because we now have all those goodies, they're unable to think their way to the next level. And that next level yields two truths: (1) Relations between Labor (those who work) and Management (those who pay for work) will always be adversarial; and (2) because Management possesses the lion's share of the wealth, resources, power, education, prestige and government patronage, Labor's only hope lies in organizing.

The Need for Big Labor

With the post–New Deal federal government having demonstrated that it is slavishly accommodating to Corporate America (despite the occasional crumb thrown labor's way), it should be apparent even to those who are uncomfortable with "collectivism" that the only entity

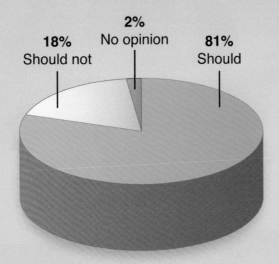

Public Support for Labor Unions

Do you think workers in this country should or should not have a right to form unions to negotiate with employers on things like working conditions, pay, benefits, and pensions?

18%
Should not

2%
No opinion

81%
Should

Taken from: *Washington Post*–ABC News Poll, March 13, 2011.

capable of taking on Big Business is Big Labor. The choice for working people is either accepting "genteel poverty," or joining together and rising up.

Corporations are predictable. They hate paying taxes; they hate paying wages (the U.S. Chamber of Commerce has spent millions lobbying against raising the minimum wage, which, even today, at $6.55, is pitifully low); they hate unions; and they more or less hate the federal government, which they view as an impediment—until they need bailouts or regulations to stifle their competitors.

Union efforts in the past have provided American workers with many benefits, including the forty-hour workweek, pensions, equal pay for women, and health insurance. These are benefits that today's unions fight to keep.

Kevin Phillips, former Republican strategist and speech writer for [former president] Richard Nixon, and author of the book, "The Politics of Rich and Poor," is no friend of labor. Far from it. But Phillips believes that citizens should be given the opportunity to prosper; and having watched in disbelief and disgust what happened during Ronald Reagan's two terms as president, he's afraid that, unless something reverses the trend, the phenomenon known as Middle-Class America will vanish forever.

> **FAST FACT**
>
> According to a 2009 study by the Center for Economic and Policy Research, the most heavily unionized age group was 55- to 64-year-olds and the least unionized age group was 16- to 24-year-olds.

What alarms Phillips is not only the "financialization" of the economy (the move away from manufacturing and into the credit industry), but the staggering gap that has developed between the wealthy and those in the middle and at the bottom. The rich are not only getting richer, they're manipulating the means by which they continue to broaden that gap.

The Relevance of Labor Unions

Which brings us back to unions. As Phillips notes, the average worker's income hasn't risen in real dollars (taking into account cost of living) since 1973. Two incomes are now required to support a standard of living previously supplied by one. Polls show that while only 12.4 per cent of the workforce is organized, close to 60 per cent of America's workers say they'd be interested in joining a union.

But why the discrepancy? Why only 12.4 per cent membership when so many more would like to join? While the abandonment of the manufacturing sector has, undoubtedly, resulted in the loss of many union jobs, Big Business is largely to blame for it. In collusion with Republicans and gutless Democrats, corporations—through stalling and intimidation tactics—have made it extremely difficult for workers to unionize.

Again, corporations are, by nature, neither altruistic nor generous. They are acquisitive. They are selfish. They are predatory. Corporations resent anything that stands in the way of making money, which is why they regard taxes as "robbery," and wages and benefits not as an investment in the workforce, but as "overhead."

And because union wages and benefits [bennies] are roughly 15-20 per cent higher than non-union wages and bennies, Corporate America dreads labor unions and does everything in its power to neutralize them. Meanwhile, that staggering gap between the rich and the rest of us continues to grow. Even hardcore Republicans are alarmed by it.

Given the direction of the country, shouldn't labor unions be seen not only as *relevant*, but as absolutely *vital?* Without the unions propping up wages and benefits, who would do it? Arguably, without unions, the U.S. would become a glorified post-industrial oligarchy.

EVALUATING THE AUTHOR'S ARGUMENTS:

In this viewpoint David Macaray suggests that labor unions keep workers out of poverty. How does Lee E. Ohanian, author of the following viewpoint, disagree with this?

Viewpoint

4

The US Economy Would Be Harmed by Increased Unionization

Lee E. Ohanian

"More unionization ... will further depress the economy."

In the following viewpoint Lee E. Ohanian argues that higher unionization rates are not the way to increase jobs and raise wages. Ohanian claims that the only way unions can have higher wages for their members is by reducing competition, which in turn reduces employment and the economic output of business, particularly in the low-wage sector. Ohanian concludes that there are better ways to promote wage growth, such as through education and training. Ohanian is professor of economics at the University of California–Los Angeles and a senior fellow at the Hoover Institution.

AS YOU READ, CONSIDER THE FOLLOWING QUESTIONS:
 1. What is the unemployment rate that the author cites as evidence of a poor economy?
 2. Ohanian claims that if unionization rates returned to 1970s levels, how many jobs would be lost?
 3. Job loss from increased unionization would fall disproportionately on which workers, according to the author?

The government's June [2010] employment report showed that the number of new private jobs continues to remain far too low to reduce unemployment from its current 9.5% rate. The pressure is mounting in Washington to get the economy on the right track. But recent decisions by President [Barack] Obama and his administration to increase unionization are steps in the wrong direction.

Efforts to Increase Unionization

These steps include executive orders that increase union bargaining power, including one that gave preference to union labor on big federal construction projects, and a recent revision of a 75-year-old National Labor Relations Board ruling that now makes it easier for airline and railroad workers to organize.

> **FAST FACT**
>
> According to the US Bureau of Labor Statistics, the US unemployment rate jumped from 5 percent or less during 2007 to over 9 percent throughout 2010.

From the beginning of his term in office Mr. Obama has made union priorities his priorities, most conspicuously by supporting the Employee Free Choice Act (EFCA). This misleadingly named bill would replace the secret ballot with a signature on a card, the so-called card check, in union elections. It would also require mediation if the union and the employer can't reach an initial union contract, and impose binding arbitration if mediation is unsuccessful.

University of California professor Lee E. Ohanian (second from right) testifies before Congress. Ohanian argues that unions raise wages by restricting competition at the expense of nonunion jobs and the economy as a whole.

EFCA is currently stalled in Congress because of the controversial card-check provision. Nevertheless, Craig Becker, whom Mr. Obama put on the National Labor Relations Board [NLRB] argued in a 1993 law review article that the NLRB can rewrite union election rules without Congressional approval. The five-member board is made up of three Democrats and two Republicans.

Unionization and Wages

Those [who] want more unionization claim it is necessary to raise wages. Instead it will further depress the economy. My research suggests that if unionization rates returned to 1970s levels (roughly in the mid 20% range of the private work force), and if new unions could achieve the same wage premium as existing unions have achieved over nonunion workplaces, then employment could decline by about 4.5 million and real GDP [gross domestic product] could fall by about $500 billion per year.

Why? Unions raise members' wages by restricting competition, much as a business monopoly raises prices by restricting competition. Economists criticize business monopolies for raising prices above what they would be in a competitive marketplace, which reduces employment and output. Unionization reduces employment and output much the same way by raising wages above underlying worker productivity.

Small businesses would be particularly impacted—about 55% of union elections occurred at businesses with 30 or fewer employees between 2003 and 2006. Negotiating costs are high for smaller firms, many of which do not have collective bargaining specialists in house. Add this cost to low profit margins, and expanding unionization presents a significant burden to these employers.

Alternatives to Higher Unionization

Worse, workers with low educational attainment and low wages will be most at risk. Research published in *Econometrica* in 2000 by myself, Per Krusell, José-Victor Ríos-Rull and Giovanni Violante suggests that rapid technological advances are making sophisticated capital goods cheap substitutes for low-skilled workers, and are an important reason why wages for these workers have declined in recent years. This means that the job loss from increased unionization will tend to fall disproportionately on the lowest-paid workers.

Americans should place a high priority on policies that raise wages and expand employment opportunities. But there are ways to do so at a fraction of the cost of higher unionization. Promoting wage growth in a competitive economy boils down to raising worker productivity. One way to do so is by increasing financial aid for education and job training.

The foundation for this positive approach already exists with Mr. Obama's $12 billion community college initiative. Increasing education and job training opportunities—not restricting competition through higher unionization—will expand incomes, increase global competitiveness, and provide opportunities for workers to succeed.

EVALUATING THE AUTHOR'S ARGUMENTS:

In this viewpoint Lee E. Ohanian argues that unionization raises wages by restricting competition, at the expense of jobs and the larger economy. Based on what he says, would a society where all workers were unionized eliminate this problem or make it worse? Explain your answer.

Attacks on Unions Have Drawn Public Sympathy

Harold Meyerson

> **"[Government anti-union action] has produced a shift in public opinion that will help America's unions."**

In the following viewpoint Harold Meyerson argues that recent attempts to limit the collective bargaining rights of public employees have backfired as Americans have responded with strong support for the collective bargaining rights of workers. Meyerson hypothesizes that the American public is largely supportive of many of the public employees who belong to unions and does not want to see the long-standing right to collective bargaining diminished. He concludes that it remains to be seen whether or not such sentiment will help labor unions on the whole. Meyerson is the editor at large of the *American Prospect* and a columnist for the *Washington Post*.

AS YOU READ, CONSIDER THE FOLLOWING QUESTIONS:

1. According to Meyerson, approximately what percentage of Americans support the collective bargaining rights of public employees?
2. What was the public's response to attempts to limit the power of unions by Governors Scott Walker and John Kasich, according to the author?
3. Meyerson says that labor unions recruited how many new members in response to the actions of Walker?

AFL-CIO [American Federation of Labor and Congress of Industrial Organizations] President Richard Trumka was only speaking truth when he called Scott Walker, Wisconsin's Republican governor, the labor movement's "Mobilizer of the Year." The backlash against Walker's successful (for now) drive to end collective bargaining for Wisconsin's public employees has been stunning in its scope, intensity, and (ongoing) duration.

The big political question is how far and how deep that backlash will go. My first guess is that it has produced a shift in public opinion that will help America's unions, though it will take a lot more than

AFL-CIO president Richard Trumka (far right) talks to Wisconsin union workers in February 2011. Trumka says that the recent Republican attacks on the unions have invigorated the US labor movement.

public sympathy to rebuild labor's power. My second guess is that it will help the Democratic Party across the industrial Midwest.

Before Wisconsin's epic battle, "who the hell knew what collective bargaining was?" asks Karen Nussbaum, who heads the AFL-CIO–affiliated organization Working America, which enrolls residents of working-class communities in union political programs. "It has way too many syllables."

But as Wisconsin's workers and their allies demonstrated day after day at the Capitol, and as the state's Democratic senators stayed away to forestall the vote, Americans' minds were concentrated on a right that certainly hadn't been in the news much for decades: the right of workers to join together to bargain with management. Within a few days of Walker's action, three national polls—*USA Today*/Gallup, *Wall Street Journal*/NBC, and *New York Times*/CBS—all showed that Americans opposed stripping public employees of their collective-bargaining rights, by roughly 60 percent to 30 percent margins.

Who knew? What with conservatives' continual demonization of public-employee unions, the support that Americans show for public employees' rights has to come as a surprise. Three factors, I believe, informed the public's judgment. The first was the demonstrations themselves, which put very human and sympathetic faces—those of teachers, nurses, cops, and firefighters—on Walker's targets. The second, which followed from the first, was that it's hard to believe that those teachers, nurses, cops, and firefighters, once you see them, are really the folks who are making out like bandits in our no-end-in-sight jobs recession.

And third, Americans aren't keen on the idea of taking away long-established rights, particularly when doing so fundamentally destabilizes the social balance of power that we take (or took) for granted. In the

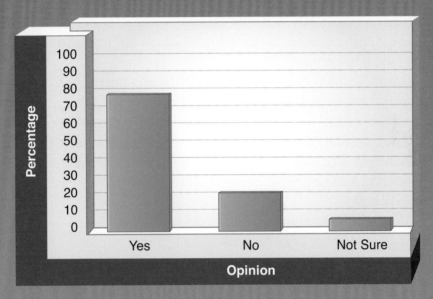

Support for Bargaining Rights

Should unionized public employees have the same right to bargain as private companies' employees?

Taken from: *Wall Street Journal*/NBC News Poll, March 2, 2011.

industrial (or post-industrial) Midwest, which was not only the stronghold for manufacturing unions but also the place where public-sector workers first won collective-bargaining rights, unions are a venerable yin to businesses' yang. Wiping them off the map, as Walker, Gov. John Kasich of Ohio, and other Republicans are trying to do, is not only undemocratic but violates every precept of Burkean [according to eighteenth-century British philosopher Edmund Burke] conservatism. Stripping Americans of their rights and uprooting the social order isn't high on the public's to-do list.

Which is why Walker, Kasich, and kindred Republican overreachers are in real trouble. Recent polls show that Walker's and Kasich's approval ratings have turned sharply negative. Moreover, as Trumka suggested, they have galvanized their opponents. In Wisconsin, the campaigns to recall Republican state senators who supported Walker's bill have out-fundraised and out-organized the Republicans' campaigns. In Ohio, Sherrod Brown, the progressive and pro-labor Democratic U.S. senator who looked to be facing a tough re-election race next year [2012] now enjoys sharply higher favorability ratings. President Barack Obama, who needs to win many Midwestern states if he's to be re-elected, would do well to follow Brown's lead and align himself more clearly with the cause of worker rights—particularly because his economic policies don't look to hold much promise for the Midwest's economic prospects.

But if Walker's overreach leads to a Democratic comeback in the nation's heartland, will it do the same for unions? Clearly, it has energized the unions' political programs and their appeal: Working America has recruited 20,000 more members in Wisconsin since the Walker wars began. But successful mass mobilizations and even clout at the ballot box don't necessarily translate into growing membership at the workplace.

While the Wisconsin backlash could restore public employees' rights, the nation's anemic labor laws still make it almost impossible for private-sector workers to organize and win contracts. Restoring workers' rights in both the public and private sectors would require, just for starters, a mobilization that would dwarf Madison's in size, intensity, and duration —and who knows what else? Labor may ultimately stanch its wounds in Wisconsin. Whether it can thrive again is still an open question.

EVALUATING THE AUTHOR'S ARGUMENTS:

In this viewpoint Harold Meyerson claims that most Americans support the collective bargaining right of public employees. Does this mean most Americans want to join a union? Why or why not?

Viewpoint

6

The Outlook for Private and Public Unions Is Bleak

Michael Barone

"The outlook for both private- and public-sector unionism is problematic."

In the following viewpoint Michael Barone argues that the labor unions in both the private and public sectors are outdated and are being rejected by voters. Barone claims that private-sector unions have been in decline for quite some time because they cripple business and are no longer needed. He contends that although public-sector unions have been growing, American voters are moving to states with fewer unions and saying no to unionization. Barone is senior political analyst for the *Washington Examiner*, a resident fellow at the American Enterprise Institute, and a Fox News Channel contributor.

AS YOU READ, CONSIDER THE FOLLOWING QUESTIONS:

1. According to Barone, for the first time in history the majority of union members work for whom?
2. What laws have been passed since the 1950s that have made unions irrelevant, according to the author?
3. What percentage of federal employees earn over one hundred thousand dollars a year, according to Barone?

Michael Barone, "Public-Sector Unions Bleed Taxpayers," *Washington Examiner*, February 7, 2010. www.washingtonexaminer.com. Copyright © 2010 by Washington Examiner. All rights reserved. Reproduced by permission.

G rowing up in Michigan in the heyday of the United Auto Workers [UAW], I long assumed that labor unions were part of the natural order of things.

That's no longer clear. Last month [January 2010] the Labor Department reported that private-sector unions lost 834,000 members last year and now represent only 7.2 percent of private-sector employees. That's down from the all-time peak of 36 percent in 1953 and '54.

But union membership is still growing in the public sector. Last year 37.4 percent of public-sector employees were union members. That percentage was down near zero in the 1950s. For the first time in history, a majority of union members are government employees.

In my view, the outlook for both private- and public-sector unionism is problematic.

Private-sector unionism is adversarial. Economic studies show that such unions do extract premium wages and benefits from employers. But that puts employers at a competitive disadvantage. Back in the 1950s, the Big Three auto companies dominated the industry and were at the top of the Fortune 500. Last year General Motors and Chrysler went bankrupt and are now owned by the government and the UAW. Ford only barely escaped.

Adversarial unionism tends to produce rigid work rules that retard adaptation and innovation. We have had a three-decade experiment pitting UAW work rules against the flexible management of Japanese- and European-owned nonunion auto firms.

The results are in. Yes, clueless management at the Detroit firms for years ignored problems with product quality and made boneheaded investment mistakes. But adversarial unionism made it much, much harder for Detroit to produce high-quality vehicles than it was for nonunionized companies.

As economist Barry Hirsch points out, nonunion manufacturing employment rose from 12 million to 14 million between 1973 and

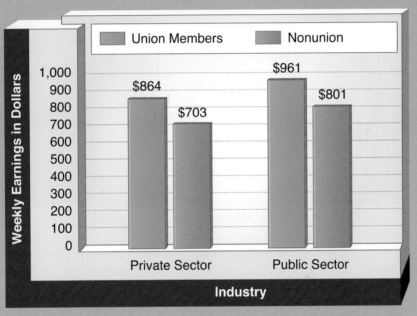

Earnings by Union Affiliation, 2010

Median weekly earnings of full-time wage and salary workers by union affiliation and industry:

Taken from: US Bureau of Labor Statistics, January 21, 2011.

2006. In those years, union manufacturing employment dropped from 8 million to 2 million. "Unionism," Hirsch writes, "is a poor fit in a dynamic, competitive economy."

Moreover, federal laws passed since the 1950s now protect workers from racial and sex discrimination, safety hazards and pension failure. They don't need unions to do this anymore.

Public-sector unionism is a very different animal from private-sector unionism. It is not adversarial but collusive. Public-sector unions strive to elect their management, which in turn can extract money from taxpayers to increase wages and benefits—and can promise pensions that future taxpayers will have to fund.

Immigrant day workers in Los Angeles talk to Laborers' International Union president Terence O'Sullivan (center, back to camera) about joining a union. Unions are courting day laborers in hopes of reversing downward trends in union membership among private-sector employees.

The results are plain to see. States such as New York, New Jersey and California, where public-sector unions are strong, now face enormous budget deficits and pension liabilities. In such states, the public sector has become a parasite sucking the life out of the private-sector economy. Not surprisingly, Americans have been steadily migrating out of such states and into states like Texas, where public-sector unions are weak and taxes are much lower.

Barack Obama is probably the most union-friendly president since Lyndon Johnson. He has obviously been unable to stop the decline of private-sector unionism. But he is doing his best to increase the power—and dues income—of public-sector unions.

One-third of last year's $787 billion stimulus package was aid to state and local governments—an obvious attempt to bolster public-sector unions. And a successful one: While the private sector has lost

7 million jobs, the number of public-sector jobs has risen. The number of federal government jobs has been increasing by 10,000 a month, and the percentage of federal employees earning over $100,000 has jumped to 19 percent during the recession.

Obama and his party are acting in collusion with unions that contributed something like $400,000,000 to Democrats in the 2008 campaign cycle. Public-sector unionism tends to be a self-perpetuating machine that extracts money from taxpayers and then puts it on a conveyor belt to the Democratic party.

But it may not turn out to be a perpetual motion machine. Public-sector employees are still heavily outnumbered by those who depend on the private sector for their livelihoods. The next Congress may not be as willing as this one has been to bail out state governments dominated by public-sector unions. Voters may bridle at the higher taxes needed to pay for $100,000-plus pensions for public employees who retire in their 50s. Or they may move, as so many have already done, to states like Texas.

Obama's Democrats have used the financial crisis to expand the public sector and the public-sector unions. But voters seem to be saying, "Enough."

EVALUATING THE AUTHOR'S ARGUMENTS:

In this viewpoint Michael Barone claims that people are rejecting unions because of the expense to states. What evidence does Harold Meyerson, author of the previous viewpoint, give that undermines Barone's claim?

Facts About Labor Unions

Editor's note: These facts can be used in reports or papers to reinforce or add credibility when making important points or claims.

Labor Union Membership in the United States
According to the US Bureau of Labor Statistics, in 2010,

- 14.7 million workers—11.9 percent of wage-earning and salaried workers—were members of unions;
- the union membership rate for public-sector workers was 36.2 percent, whereas the membership rate for private-sector workers was 6.9 percent;
- 13.4 percent of African American workers, 11.7 percent of white workers, 10.9 percent of Asian workers, and 10 percent of Hispanic workers were members of unions;
- 12.6 percent of male workers and 11.1 percent of female workers were members of unions;
- eight states had union membership rates below 5 percent—North Carolina (3.2 percent), Arkansas, Georgia (4 percent each), Louisiana (4.3 percent), Mississippi (4.5 percent), South Carolina, Virginia (4.6 percent each), and Tennessee (4.7 percent);
- Six states had union membership rates of more than 17 percent: New York (24.2 percent), Alaska (22.9 percent), Hawaii (21.8 percent), Washington (19.4 percent), California (17.5 percent), and New Jersey (17.1 percent).

Earnings and Benefits of Workers
Represented by Labor Unions
According to the US Bureau of Labor Statistics, in 2010,

- union members had median weekly earnings of $917, while those who were not represented by unions had median weekly earnings of $717;
- male union members had median weekly earnings of $967, whereas male workers not represented by a union had median weekly earnings of $789;

- female union members had median weekly earnings of $856, whereas female workers not represented by a union had median weekly earnings of $639;
- white male union members had the highest median weekly earnings of $985, whereas Hispanic female workers not represented by a union had the lowest median weekly earnings of $489.

According to the Center for Economic and Policy Research, in 2008,
- 80.1 percent of union workers had health insurance, compared with 55.8 percent of nonunion workers;
- 76 percent of union workers had a retirement plan, compared with 45 percent of nonunion workers.

Americans' Views on Labor Unions

According to a nationwide poll taken by Gallup in 2011,
- 52 percent of Americans approve of labor unions, but 42 percent disapprove of them;
- 78 percent of Democrats expressed approval compared with 26 percent of Republicans and 52 percent of Independents;
- 73 percent of those living in union households approved of labor unions, whereas only 48 percent of those in nonunion households approved of them;
- 55 percent of Americans think labor unions will become weaker in the future, 22 percent think they will stay the same, and 20 percent think they will be stronger in the future;
- 42 percent of Americans said they personally would like to see labor unions have less influence in the future, 30 percent said they would like to see more influence, and 25 percent would like unions of the future to have the same amount of influence.

According to a nationwide survey by the Pew Research Center for the People & the Press,
- in 2010, 42 percent had an unfavorable opinion of labor unions, whereas 41 percent had a favorable opinion;
- In 2009, 61 percent said that labor unions are necessary to protect the working person, whereas 34 percent disagreed that they are necessary.

Organizations to Contact

The editors have compiled the following list of organizations concerned with the issues debated in this book. The descriptions are derived from materials provided by the organizations. All have publications or information available for interested readers. The list was compiled on the date of publication of the present volume; the information provided here may change. Be aware that many organizations take several weeks or longer to respond to inquiries, so allow as much time as possible for the receipt of requested materials.

Alliance for Worker Freedom (AWF)
722 Twelfth St. NW, 4th Fl., Washington, DC 20005
(202) 785-0266 • fax: (202) 785-0261
e-mail: info@workerfreedom.org
website: www.workerfreedom.org

AWF is a nonpartisan organization dedicated to combating antiworker legislation and to promoting free markets. AWF uses research, education, and lobbying efforts to protect workers' rights and to advocate for freer and more transparent economic systems. AWF provides research at its website, including the 2009 *Index of Worker Freedom*, comparing worker freedom in the states.

American Enterprise Institute for Public Policy Research (AEI)
1150 Seventeenth St. NW, Washington, DC 20036
(202) 862-5800 • fax: (202) 862-7177
e-mail: webmaster@aei.org
website: www.aei.org

AEI is a community of scholars and supporters committed to expanding liberty, increasing individual opportunity, and strengthening free enterprise. AEI's purpose is to serve leaders and the public through research and education on the most important issues of the day in the areas of economics, culture, politics, foreign affairs, and national defense. AEI publishes the *American,* a variety of AEI outlook papers, and studies such as "A Better Bargain: Overhauling Teacher Collective Bargaining for the 21st Century."

American Federation of Labor and Congress of Industrial Organizations (AFL-CIO)

815 Sixteenth St. NW, Washington, DC 20006
(202) 637-5000
website: www.aflcio.org

The AFL-CIO is a voluntary federation of fifty-six national and international labor unions, representing 12.2 million members. The AFL-CIO educates union members about issues that affect the daily lives of working families and encourages them to make their voices heard by government. The AFL-CIO has numerous publications available at its website, including "Why You Need a Union."

American Rights at Work

1616 P St. NW, Ste. 150, Washington, DC 20036
(202) 822-2127 • fax: (202) 822-2168
e-mail: info@americanrightsatwork.org
website: www.americanrightsatwork.org

American Rights at Work is a nonprofit advocacy organization dedicated to promoting the freedom of workers to organize unions and bargain collectively with employers. American Rights at Work investigates workers' rights abuses, promotes public policy that protects workers, and publicizes success stories of companies that respect workers' rights. American Rights at Work publishes reports, case studies, issue briefs, and educational materials based on original research, such as "Businesses and Communities Benefit When Workers Have Unions."

Cato Institute

1000 Massachusetts Ave. NW, Washington, DC 20001
(202) 842-0200 • fax: (202) 842-3490
website: www.cato.org

The Cato Institute is a public-policy research organization dedicated to the principles of individual liberty, limited government, free markets, and peace. The institute is dedicated to increasing and enhancing the understanding of key public policies and to realistically analyzing their impact on the principles identified above. The Cato Institute publishes many publications, such as the *Cato Journal*, with articles including "Unions, Protectionism, and US Competitiveness."

Center for American Progress
1333 H St. NW, 10th Fl., Washington, DC 20005
(202) 682-1611 • fax: (202) 682-1867
website: www.americanprogress.org

The Center for American Progress is a nonprofit, nonpartisan organization dedicated to improving the lives of Americans through progressive ideas and action. The center dialogues with leaders, thinkers, and citizens to explore the vital issues facing America and the world. The organization publishes numerous research papers, which are available at its website, including, "Unions Make the Middle Class: Without Unions, the Middle Class Withers."

Center for Economic and Policy Research (CEPR)
1611 Connecticut Ave. NW, Ste. 400, Washington, DC 20009
(202) 293-5380 • fax: (202) 588-1356
e-mail: cepr@cepr.net
website: www.cepr.net

CEPR aims to promote democratic debate on the most important economic and social issues that affect people's lives. It conducts both professional research and public education and provides briefings and testimony to Congress and reports for the general public, including "Downturn Continues to Lower Union Membership."

Economic Policy Institute (EPI)
1333 H St. NW, Ste. 300, East Tower, Washington, DC 20005-4707
(202) 775-8810 • fax: (202) 775-0819
e-mail: epi@epi.org
website: www.epi.org

EPI is a nonprofit think tank that seeks to broaden the discussion about economic policy to include the interests of low- and middle-income workers. EPI briefs policy makers at all levels of government; provides technical support to national, state, and local activists and community organizations; testifies before national, state, and local legislatures; and provides information and background to the print and electronic media. It publishes books, studies, issue briefs, popular education materials, and other publications, among which is the biennially published *State of Working America.*

Institute for America's Future (IAF)

1825 K St. NW, Ste. 400, Washington, DC 20006
(202) 955-5665 • fax: (202) 955-5606
website: http://institute.ourfuture.org

IAF works to equip Americans with the tools and information needed to drive issues in the national debate, challenge what it sees as failed conservative policies, and build support for its progressive vision of a government that is on the side of working people. Drawing on a network of scholars, activists, and leaders across the country, IAF develops policy ideas, educational materials, and outreach programs. Publications of IAF include "America Is Strong When Our Unions Are Strong."

National Right to Work Legal Defense Foundation

8001 Braddock Rd., Springfield, VA 22160
(800) 336-3600 • fax: (703) 321-9613
website: www.nrtw.org

The National Right to Work Legal Defense Foundation is a nonprofit organization that defends the right to work for a living without being compelled to belong to a union. The National Right to Work Legal Defense Foundation provides free legal aid to employees whose human or civil rights have been violated by abuses of compulsory unionism. The National Right to Work Legal Defense Foundation publishes a newsletter, *Foundation Action,* as well as publishing news stories on its website.

For Further Reading

Books

Ashby, Steven K., and C.J. Hawking. *Staley: The Fight for a New American Labor Movement.* Urbana: University of Illinois Press, 2009. Chronicles the labor conflict in the mid-1990s at the A.E. Staley corn processing plant in Illinois, where workers waged one of the most hard-fought struggles in recent labor history.

Bennett, James T., and Bruce E. Kaufman, eds. *What Do Unions Do?: A Twenty-Year Perspective.* New Brunswick, NJ: Transaction, 2007. Argues that on the basis of the economic and sociopolitical effects of labor unions, unions are, on balance, beneficial for the economy and society.

Cobble, Dorothy Sue, ed. *The Sex of Class: Women Transforming American Labor.* Ithaca, NY: Cornell University Press, 2007. Analyzes how the sex of workers matters in understanding the jobs they do, the problems they face, and the new labor movements they are creating.

Dine, Philip M. *State of the Unions: How Labor Can Strengthen the Middle Class, Improve Our Economy, and Regain Political Influence.* New York: McGraw-Hill, 2008. Provides an account of labor's decline through firsthand narratives of employees and the decline's meaning for US politics and the middle class.

Dray, Philip. *There Is Power in a Union: The Epic Story of Labor in America.* New York: Doubleday, 2010. Argues that the accomplishments of organized labor in the twentieth century illuminate its central role in America's social, political, economic, and cultural evolution.

Dubofsky, Melvyn, and Foster Rhea Dulles. *Labor in America: A History.* Wheeling, IL: Harlan Davidson, 2010. Provides an account of the history of worker and labor movements in the United States.

Early, Steve. *The Civil Wars in US Labor: Birth of a New Workers' Movement or Death Throes of the Old?* Chicago: Haymarket, 2011. Explores the disputes about union structure, membership rights, organizing strategy, and contract standards that occurred within the US labor movement between 2008 and 2010.

Fletcher Jr., Bill, and Fernando Gapasin. *Solidarity Divided: The Crisis in Organized Labor and a New Path Toward Social Justice*. Berkeley and Los Angeles: University of California Press, 2008. Critically examines organized labor's current crisis, calling for a reexamination of the ideological and structural underpinnings of the labor movement.

Frymer, Paul. *Black and Blue: African Americans, the Labor Movement, and the Decline of the Democratic Party*. Princeton, NJ: Princeton University Press, 2008. Explores the politics and history that led to the racial integration of organized labor, contending that the Democratic Party ultimately sowed the seeds of its decline.

Getman, Julius G. *Restoring the Power of Unions: It Takes a Movement*. New Haven, CT: Yale University Press, 2010. Argues that a resurgent labor movement is possible if unions return to their historical roots as a social movement.

Leef, George C. *Free Choice for Workers: A History of the Right to Work Movement*. New York: Jameson, 2010. Argues that there has been a struggle between the bosses of organized labor and Americans opposed to what the authors claim is their coercive power for fifty years.

Moe, Terry M. *Special Interest: Teachers Unions and America's Public Schools*. Washington, DC: Brookings Institution Press, 2011. Argues that as long as the teachers' unions remain powerful, the nation's schools will never be organized to provide kids with the most effective education possible.

Moody, Kim. *US Labor in Trouble and Transition: The Failure of Reform from Above, the Promise of Revival from Below*. New York: Verso, 2007. Tells the story of union decline in America, arguing that the rise of immigrant labor and its efforts at self-organization can reenergize unions from below.

Paige, Rod. *The War Against Hope: How Teachers' Unions Hurt Children, Hinder Teachers, and Endanger Public Education*. Nashville: Thomas Nelson, 2007. Contends that teachers' unions are selfishly shackling students to a failing education system, terrorizing teachers, students, and their parents.

Schiavone, Michael. *Unions in Crisis?: The Future of Organized Labor in America.* Westport, CT: Praeger, 2008. Arguing that a strong union movement is needed now more than ever, outlines the major changes unions need to make to revitalize the US labor movement.

Skurzynski, Gloria. *Sweat and Blood: A History of US Labor Unions.* Minneapolis: Twenty-First Century Books, 2008. Using many examples, gives a history of how working people formed labor unions in an attempt to gain fair wages, reasonable hours, and secure lives.

van Elteren, Mel. *Labor and the American Left: An Analytical History.* Jefferson, NC: McFarland, 2011. Explores relations between organized labor and left-wing parties and movements in America at crucial junctures from the 1870s to the present.

Yates, Michael D. *Why Unions Matter.* New York: Monthly Review Press, 2009. Arguing that workers need unions, explains how unions are formed, how they operate, how collective bargaining works, and what unions have done to bring workers together.

Periodicals and Internet Sources

AFL-CIO. "The Facts: Union Representation and the NLRA," December 2008. www.aflcio.org.

Bacon, David. "Equality and Rights for Immigrants—the Key to Organizing Unions," *Monthly Review*, October 2010.

Barone, Michael. "Public Unions Force Taxpayers to Fund Democrats," *Washington Examiner*, February 23, 2011.

Barro, Robert J. "Unions vs. The Right to Work," *Wall Street Journal*, February 28, 2011.

Bethell, Tom. "Labor Unions and the News Media," *American Spectator*, December 2009–January 2010.

Bowman, Karlyn. "Labor Unions Lag in Power," *Forbes*, March 20, 2009.

Cameron, Bruce N. "Labor Unions and Workers' Rites," *Liberty*, January/February 2010.

Cooper, Michael, and Megan Thee-Brenan. "Majority in Poll Back Employees in Public Sector Unions," *New York Times*, February 28, 2011.

Coulson, Andrew J. "A Less Perfect Union," *American Spectator*, June 2011.

DeHaven, Tad. "Recession of 2008 Exposed True Cost of Public Employee Unions," *Washington Examiner*, March 22, 2011.

Dinardo, John. "Still Open for Business: Unionization Has No Causal Effect on Firm Closures," Economic Policy Institute Briefing Paper, March 20, 2009. www.epi.org.

Drum, Kevin. "Plutocracy Now: What Wisconsin Is Really About," *Mother Jones*, March/April 2011.

Dubofsky, Melvyn. "Does Labor Have a Future?," *New Leader*, January/February 2010.

Elk, Mike. "The Revival of Labor," *American Prospect*, March 4, 2011.

Featherstone, Liza. "Fighting Back," *American Prospect*, April 13, 2011.

Ferrara, Peter. "Card Check Means Union Slavery," *American Spectator*, March 25, 2009.

Gingrich, Newt. "Arbitration the Real Threat in EFCA," *Politico*, April 22, 2009.

Goldberg, Jonah. "Public Unions Must Go," *National Review*, February 23, 2011.

Griswold, Daniel. "Unions, Protectionism, and US Competitiveness," *Cato Journal*, Winter 2010.

Hentoff, Nat. "Teacher Unions vs. Poor Kids," Real Clear Politics, March 28, 2009. www.realclearpolitics.com.

Hess, Frederick M. "The Big Payback," *The Daily*, February 23, 2011. www.thedaily.com.

Karlsson, Stefan. "The Case Against Unions: They Kill Jobs," *Christian Science Monitor*, July 31, 2010.

Lichtenstein, Nelson, and Erin Johansson. "Creating Hourly Careers: A New Vision for Walmart and the Country," American Rights at Work, January 2011. www.americanrightsatwork.org.

Mantell, Ruth. "US Workers' Salaries Lost Ground in Past Decade," *Wall Street Journal*, July 7, 2010.

Meyerson, Harold. "Why Can't Labor Get a Little More Help from Its Friends?," *American Prospect*, April 6, 2010.

Moberg, David. "Unions Work to Turn the Tide," *In These Times*, July 2011.

Murdock, Deroy. "The Right to Choose: It's Time for the National Right to Work Act," *National Review*, March 11, 2011.

Orr, Andrea. "Scapegoating Public Sector Workers," Economic Policy Institute, March 8, 2011. www.epi.org.

Pawlenty, Tim. "Government Unions vs. Taxpayers," *Wall Street Journal*, December 13, 2010.

Payne, Michael. "Unionization: A Private Sector Solution to the Economic Crisis," *Dissent*, Spring 2009.

Pollin, Robert, and Jeffrey Thompson. "The Betrayal of Public Workers," *Nation*, March 7–14, 2011.

Root, Damon W. "Whitewashing the History of Organized Labor," *Reason*, February 23, 2011.

Schwartz, Stephen. "Which Side Are They On?: American Labor Unions and How They Got That Way," *Weekly Standard*, April 5, 2010.

Sherk, James. "Do Americans Today Still Need Labor Unions? No: Labor Unions Add to Costs and Discourage Productivity," *Fredericksburg (VA) Free-Lance Star*, March 30, 2008.

Summers, Nick. "The Future of the American Worker," *Newsweek*, June 3, 2009.

Wall Street Journal, "Giving Workers a Union Choice," February 2, 2010.

Yoshikane, Akito. "The Folly of 'Right to Work' Legislation," *In These Times*, March 9, 2011.

Yoshikane, Akito. "Labor Unions a Key to Happiness, New Report Says," *In These Times*, October 7, 2010.

Websites

Bureau of Labor Statistics (www.bls.gov). This website of the US Department of Labor contains statistics about labor union membership in the United States.

National Labor Relations Board (www.nlrb.gov). This website of the independent federal agency charged with protecting employees' collective bargaining rights contains fact sheets, news, and information about its labor dispute decisions.

Unions.org (www.unions.org). This website maintains a database of over fifteen thousand union organizations across the United States.

Index

A

Acuff, Stewart, 37
AFL-CIO (American Federation of Labor and Congress of Industrial Organizations), 8, 57, 72, 81, 97–98
African Americans, 13, 15
AFSCME (American Federation of State, County, and Municipal Employees), 45
Agency-shop policy, 8
American Postal Workers Union (APWU), 97
American Spectator (magazine), 90
APWU (American Postal Workers Union), 97
Automakers, US
  federal assistance for, 100
  have lost ground to foreign competitors, 95–96
  unionization has hurt, 116

B

Baker, Dean, 66
Bandow, Doug, 79
Barone, Michael, 115
Barro, Robert, 30
Becker, Craig, 13, 107
BLS. *See* Bureau of Labor Statistics, US
Boeing Company, NLRB complaint against, 9

Boston Globe (newspaper), 31
Branstad, Terry, 89
Bronars, Stephen, 44–47
Brown, Sherrod, 114
Bureau of Labor Statistics, US (BLS)
  on decline in union membership, 91
  on median earnings of union *vs.* nonunion workers, 31
  on total union membership, 44
  on unemployment rate, 106
  on union membership rate 43, 90
Burke, Edmund, 113
Bush, George W./Bush administration, 21–22, 73
Bush, Jeb, 90

C

Card check, 37, 41, 81–83, 98, 106–107
Cartels, 24, 26
Census Bureau, US, 74
Center for Economic and Policy Research, 103
Chamber of Commerce, US, 38, 76, 102
Christie, Chris, *87*
Cohen, Donald, 90
Collective bargaining
  definition of, 51

is a right, 46–60
states should repeal in public
  sector, 50–55
Copyright, 68–69
Corporations
  labor unions are needed to
    counteract power of, 76–77,
    99–104
  unions limit efficiency of,
    94–95, 108

D
Davis-Bacon Act, 39–40
Democratic Party
  support of Employee Free
    Choice Act by, 82
  union contributions to, 37,
    91, 119
Department of Labor, US,
  116

E
Earnings/wages
  of CEOs *vs.* lowest paid
    employees, 60
  in private *vs.* public sectors,
    91–92, *117*
  raising worker productivity
    promotes growth in, 108
  stagnation in, 21
  of unionized *vs.* nonunionized
    workers, 31, 104
Econometrica (journal), 108
Economic Policy Institute,
  69
Economy(ies)
  labor unions harm, 23–28

state, labor unions do not
  harm, 29–35
state, public sector unions
  harm, 117
US, would be harmed by
  increase in unionization,
  105–109
Edwards, Chris, 50
EFCA. *See* Employee Free
  Choice Act
Employee Free Choice Act
  (EFCA, proposed), 13, 37, 38,
  98, 106–107
  should be passed, 72–78
  should not be passed, 79–84
  support for, *75, 81*
Employment
  in manufacturing, by union
    status, *25,* 116–117
  state/local government, union
    shares of, *54*
  See also Unemployment/
    unemployment rate
Europe, state of unions in, 47,
  48

F
Fine, Janice, 91
Fletcher, Bill, Jr., 91
Florida, Richard, 29
Freedom of association,
  collective bargaining and,
  54–55
Freeman, Richard, 31

G
Galbraith, John Kenneth, 77

Ghosh, Palash R., 42
Gingrich, Newt, 90
Globalization, role in decline in union membership, 45–47
Good Morning America (TV program), 30
Great Recession (2007–2009), 97
  jump in unemployment rate from, 106
Griswold, Daniel, 93

H
Hacker, Jacob S., 31
Harkin, Tom, *77*
Hirsch, Barry, 95

I
Income
  inequality in, 33, 103
  median, in 1973 *vs.* 2010, 74
  See also Earnings/wages
In the Public Interest, 90

J
Jobs
  growth of, *95*
  unions decrease numbers of, 25–26
Johnson, Dave, 17
Johnson, Lyndon, 118
Johnson, Randel, 38

K
Kasich, John, 89, 113–114
Keizer, Garrett, 56
Krusell, Per, 108

L
Labor unions
  Americans recognizing benefits of, 17–22
  are needed to counteract big business, 76–77, 99–104
  attacks on, 110–114
  decertification of, 83
  decline of, 93–98
  definition of, 7
  do not harm state economies, 29–35
  harm overall economy, 23–28
  have become less influential, 42–48
  have tremendous political influence, 36–41
  increase worker productivity, 74–76, 94
  political war is being waged to eliminate, 86–92
  positive attitudes toward, 11–16
  positive impacts of, 43, 76, 100
  See also Private sector unions; Public sector unions; Unionization
Lincoln, Abraham, 18
Lincoln, Blanche, 46

M
Macaray, David, 99
Manufacturing
  decline of, 47
  decline of union membership in, 45
  employment in, *25,* 116–117

McAlevey, Jane, 86
McConnell, Mitch, *82*
Media, 17, 20, 65, 87
Mellander, Charlotta, 33
Meyerson, Harold, 110
Miller, George, *77*
Miller, Peyton R., 36
Minimum wage, 102

N
National Labor Relations Act
  (NLRA, 1935), 7–8, 46, 52
National Labor Relations Board
  (NLRB), 7, 9, 37–38, 82, 107
  on union decertifications, 83
National Right to Work
  Committee, 8
New York Times (newspaper),
  30
NLRA (National Labor
  Relations Act, 1935), 7–8, 46,
  52
NLRB. *See* National Labor
  Relations Board
Norquist, Grover, 90–91
Nussbaum, Karen, 112

O
Obama, Barack/Obama
  administration, *39,* 90, 97–98,
  114, 118
  amount requested for aid to
    states by, 41
  community college initiative
    of, 108–109
  efforts to increase
    unionization, 106

pro-labor regulatory initiatives
  of, 38–40
Ohanian, Lee E., 105, *107*
Ohio Federation of Teachers,
  32
OPEC (Organization of
  Petroleum Exporting
  Countries), 24, 26
Opinion polls. *See* Surveys
Organization of Petroleum
  Exporting Countries (OPEC),
  24, 26
Orwell, George, 60
O'Sullivan, Terence, *118*
Ott, Ed, 91

P
Pawlenty, Tim, 91–92
Pew Research Center, 15
Phillips, Kevin, 103
Pierson, Paul, 31
PLAs (Project Labor
  Agreements), 89
Political influence
  labor unions are losing, 46–47
  labor unions are not losing,
    36–41
Polls. *See* Surveys
Postal Service, US, 96–97
President's Council of
  Economic Advisors, 74
Private sector unions
  decline in membership of, 44
  outlook is bleak for, 115–119
Privatization, of public
  assets/services, 90
Productivity

labor unions increase, 74–76, 94

raising, 108

Project Labor Agreements (PLAs), 89

Public sector unions
  cost of, to states, 53–54
  growth in, 15, 34
  harm state economies, 117
  outlook is bleak for, 115–119
  support for efforts to weaken collective bargaining by, 19

R

Railway Labor Act (1926), 38

Reagan, Ronald, 103

Reagan Revolution, 21–22

Republican Party
  efforts to deny collective bargaining to public employees, 51–52
  efforts to promote right-to-work laws, 62–63, 67
  opposition to antiunion efforts of, 113–114
  opposition to Employee Free Choice Act by, 82
  unions are political enemies of, 65

Right-to-work laws, 8
  aim to reduce bargaining power of workers, 66–71
  number of states with, 62
  protect workers from forced unionization, 61–65
  states with, *64*

Ríos-Rull, José-Victor, 108

S

Sherk, James, 23

State(s)
  change in unionization by, *34*
  collective bargaining for public employees and, 53
  government employment in, union shares of, *54*
  labor unions do not harm economies of, 29–35
  with right-to-work laws, 53, 64
  unionization rates and, 116

Surveys
  on approval of labor unions, 12, *14*, 15, *44*
  on compensation of public-sector employees, *59*
  on desire among US workers for unionization, 73, 103
  on Employee Free Choice Act, *75, 81*
  on ending collective bargaining rights, 19, *20*, 112
  on future of labor unions, 45
  on privacy of worker's vote on unionization, 80
  on support for bargaining rights for public employees, *113*
  on support for labor unions, *101*
  of union members, on job growth, *95*

T

Taft-Hartley Act (1947), 8

Toner, Paul, 30–31
Trumka, Richard, 41, *111*, 114
Two-labors fallacy, 57–58

U
UAW (United Auto Workers),
    14, 26, 28, 96
Unemployment/unemployment
    rate, 12, 18, 31, 33, 48, 76,
    106
    unionization not correlated
        with, 33
*Union Density and Economic
    Performance* (Freeman), 31
Unionization
    among private-sector workers,
        80
    reasons for decline in, 32
    in states with/without right-to-
        work laws, 69
    US economy would be harmed
        by increase in, 105–109
    variation among states in levels
        of, 31–33
Union-shop policy, 8
United Auto Workers (UAW),
    14, 26–28, 39, 47, 96, 100,
    116

V
Violante, Giovanni, 108

W
Wages. *See* Earnings/wages;
    Income
Wagner Act. *See* National Labor
    Relations Act

Walker, Bruce, 61
Walker, Scott, 30, *49*, 87, 112,
    113–114
    protest of, *19*
    recall action against, 111–112
Wall Street Journal (newspaper),
    30, 91–92
Washington Post (newspaper),
    31
Wilson, J. Justin, 40
Wisconsin
    move to limit collective
        bargaining rights in, 19, 21,
        30, 51, 87
    unionization rate in, 31, 33
Worker productivity
    labor unions increase, 74–76
Workers
    benefits gained by labor
        unions for, 43, 76, 100
    median earnings of, 31
    percentage wanting union
        representation, 73, 103
    rate of unionization among,
        43, 80, 90
    right-to-work laws aim to
        reduce bargaining power of,
        66–71
    right-to-work laws protect
        from forced unionization,
        61–65
    unions are no longer needed
        to protect, 117
Working America, 112, 114

Y
Yoshikane, Akito, 11

Picture Credits

AP Images/Andy Manis, 111
AP Images/Columbus Dispatch/Fred Squillante, 32
AP Images/Damian Dovarganes, 118
AP Images/The Eagle-Gazette, Abigail S. Fisher, 102
AP Images/EagleHerald, Rick Gebhard, 52
AP Images/Eric Gay, 96
AP Images/Haraz N. Ghanbari, 107
AP Images/Keith Srakocic, 10
AP Images/Lauren Victoria Burke, 13
AP Images/Mel Evans, 87
AP Images/M.P. King, Wisconsin State Journal, 49
AP Images/Paul Sancya, 27
AP Images/Susan Walsh, 77
AP Images/Wisconsin State Journal, John Hart, 19
© Bettmann/Corbis, 46
Bill Clarke/Roll Call/Getty Images, 82
Gale/Cengage Learning, 14, 20, 25, 34, 44, 54, 59, 64, 75, 81, 95, 101, 113, 117
© Richard Levine/Alamy, 85
Saul Loeb/AFP/Getty Images, 39
Joe Raedle/Getty Images, 58
© Stock Connection Distribution/Alamy, 63
© Jim West/Alamy, 70